THE YOSEF CODES

Sacred Geometry Mandalas

Jason Quitt

ATTENTION:

The information provided herein has been spiritually channeled and refined over many years of practice. This content is shared publicly for informational purposes only.

The meditations, practices and techniques described herein are not intended to be used as an alternative or substitute for professional medical treatment and care. This book does not attempt to give any medical diagnosis, treatment, prescription or remedial recommendations in relation to any human disease, ailment, suffering, or physical or mental condition whatsoever. Anyone who undertakes these practices on the basis of this book does so entirely at his or her own risk.

ISBN-13: 978-1543279023

ISBN-10: 1543279023

Table of Contents

Forward

By Pat Prevost, Canadian Society of Dowsers.

I suspect that all ancient symbols of sacred geometry are a simplified expression of daily living in a world devoid of the affect of modern living. What is sacred geometry? For lack of a more expansive term, it is our sensory connection, the visual, audio, and often tactile expression of the human mind as it experiences the natural physical world. The symbols and meaning that are generated from this process reflect our human attempts to design a working language with our natural world based in co-creativity.

Not all of humanity seeks co-creation with all peoples, all creatures and all places on earth. Alchemists however, do. Alchemy is a path where students of life seek to become masters of life, knowing full well that it is the study of life that makes them by default both the eternal student and the master of this special personal quest. They are cognizant that when they are gone, there will be someone else who takes up the path to divine the knowledge of the natural world.

In the world of nature we find the designs of our sacred expressions in the spiral of a sea shell, in the fractal branching pattern of a tree and in the incredible uniqueness of each snowflake. We copy these forms in attempts to reveal and to enact the life found in them. As children we doodle, creating repeating or complex patterns often dismissed by parents as mere mimicry of designs that we'd seen before. We have not only seen them before but we are them, as each design is built into the planet. And as we are from this place, each design is also built into us.

Years ago I was gifted with the Yosef Codes. As a dowser, I walk the path of discovery using time honored intuitive ways to experience the world in a deeper and co-creative way. I seek to balance and to stabilize every practice of my craft. Each new skill that I endeavor to learn and to master, I wish it to become a cherished companion on my journey here.

In my work as a dowser, I had amassed a huge library of ancient symbols which I did readily use. Then along came the Codes. They seamlessly set pace with me to promptly become trusted companions on my way. They feel complete unto themselves, very definitive about their abilities and grounded in their presence to this time... yet it is as if they have been here all along.

There is no great mystery as to how any symbol, ancient or modern, is born. The common thread that is required however is that it takes one who studies and walks the path of a student of life here on our Great Mother to bring such symbols into this existence. Jason is just such a person who by virtue of his deep natural curiosity, his playful open nature and his uniquely creative spirit has gifted to us the Codes. In this edition, Jason freely opens a door for us to guide us back to our natural right of ceremony.

I believe that the Codes will walk with you on your road of discovery very skillfully unearthing your mundane experiences to raise them to new levels of observation and understanding, bringing awareness and wisdom that will both delight and enlighten you. The Codes are in us and now we can see them. The visual design that Jason has brought to them allows a focal point for our capable mind. This union is intended to be creative, intuitive and to take us further into the very heartbeat of existence. See you there.

Introduction

When I started my shamanic healing practice in 2007, many of my first clients where friends and students whom I met during my time at the 8th Fire School of Algonquin Shamanism. Most of these clients were healers in their own right and very intuitive.

While working on them, they would describe very interesting personal experiences they would perceive during a typical healing session. On more then one occasion they would share that they could intuitively see me placing sacred geometry codes into their bodies and feeling their effects. Personally I was unaware of any of this taking place. I was merely practicing and applying what I had learned in school.

This new information about my healing style drew my curiosity because it was something that I could not see myself, yet many people I was working with were telling me that they could perceive this type of work taking place. Even on one occasion at a healing workshop a young lady approached me and said "I've never seen an energetic field like yours before, where are you from?"

I obviously didn't know how to respond to such a question, so I asked her to describe what she was seeing. She then went on to describe my energetic fields as being highly crystallized in geometric forms with sacred geometry symbols going in and out of my fields. Hearing this from a complete stranger really verified what my intuitive clients were telling me all along.

This new information I was learning about myself through personal experiences really peaked my interest in the subject. This forced me to look deeper into who I am and what was the meaning of these sacred geometric codes and energies around me.

The first thing I did was jump right into the subject and study of sacred geometry. Over the next year I tried to understand the language of sacred geometry, how it applies to energetic systems through form, sound, color, dimensions, degrees, rotation, and so on. This opened up new ways of thinking and made me look at the world with a fresh new understanding.

The next step for me was to figure out a way to translate these sacred geometric energies into something that I could express physically in this world. Eventually with the help of my guides I was able to crack the code and mathematically translate these energies into sacred geometry symbols. This is how the "The Yosef Codes" were born.

From my understanding of sacred geometry, the codes represent pictorial systems of consciousness that vibrate in resonance with different energetic systems. Our senses see it as a drawing, diagram, or design, but they really represent living vibrations of matter that extends far beyond us and out into the universe.

The codes you see in this book represent the micro level, like one cell which extends and connects to a vast body of consciousness beyond time and space.

This is why the Egyptians were always depicting the rays coming down from the sun, because the rays represented the vibrational nature of the infinite consciousness filtering down to us at the micro level.

When I asked a highly intuitive teacher what these codes do, they tuned into their higher consciousness and channeled this answer to me. "The energies of these codes have the ability to change the atmosphere where they are and affect anything around them by the laws of their vibrational nature. The codes herein were a sacred gift given to share with those that are drawn to these energetic systems.

Through these sacred geometric designs of consciousness may we reconnect to our own divine nature, and assist those on the path of returning to who we were always meant to be."

How to use:

The codes can be used in many different ways, here is a list of the most common ways they can be used.

1.) They can be scanned or photocopied for personal use.

2.) The codes can be meditated on like a Mandala or Medicine Wheel.

3.) They can be place directly on the body or chakras.

4.) To connect with the energies directly, place hand over code for at least 20 seconds, then place hand over body, chakras, food, water, etc.

5.) Place code under glass of water, food or crystal to program the energies of the codes within.

6.) Place code on a wall, in a room, under a bed, healing room, workplace, or under a pillow to broadcast the information into that space.

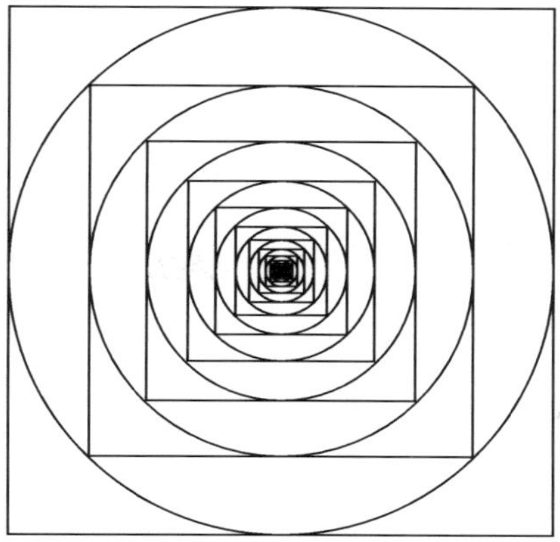

Squaring the Circle:
Introduction to Sacred Geometry

Symbol of the Masonic Square & Compass

The square and circle are the fundamental basis of all geometry and mathematics. The ancient order of the Masons still use the symbol of the square and the compass to express the great mystery and connection between geometry, the physical world and the divine.

The circle represents the infinite and divine. The square represented the finite and physical. The great geometers throughout history were searching for a way to square the circle. To square the circle meant for them to bridge the gap between the physical and the divine so that the mysteries of creation will be revealed. This was the great mystery that opened up the keys to understanding the connection between the physical world and the divine order of creation.

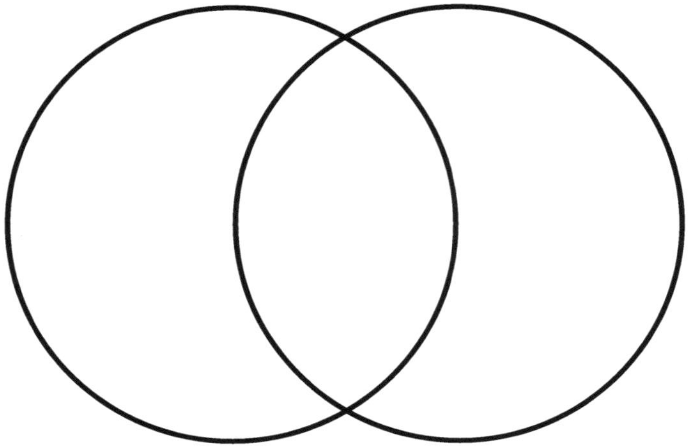

Geometry of the Vesica Piscis:

Just as cells divide, the one becomes two. This is the first step in creation and the can be visually expressed through the geometry of the Vesica Piscis. This symbol represents creation, duality, and holds within it the keys of time, space, mathematics, frequency, and harmonics.

It is through the Vesica Piscis that we can create the geometry of the 51.83 degree triangle. This triangle can be found in ancient architecture and holds the key to many secrets. The ancient geometers, mathematicians, alchemists and mystics knew that these patterns held a divine energy and had a direct connection to creation itself.

It is no mistake that the great pyramid of Giza and many others around the world are designed to be in exact harmonic with the 51.83 degree angle. This gives us a 7x11 height and width ratio of this triangle.

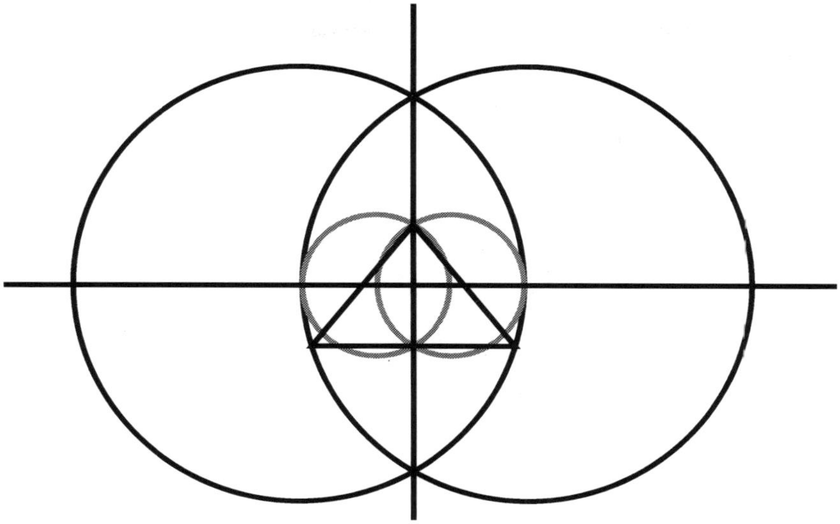

Creating the 51.83 degree triangle using a Vesica Piscis

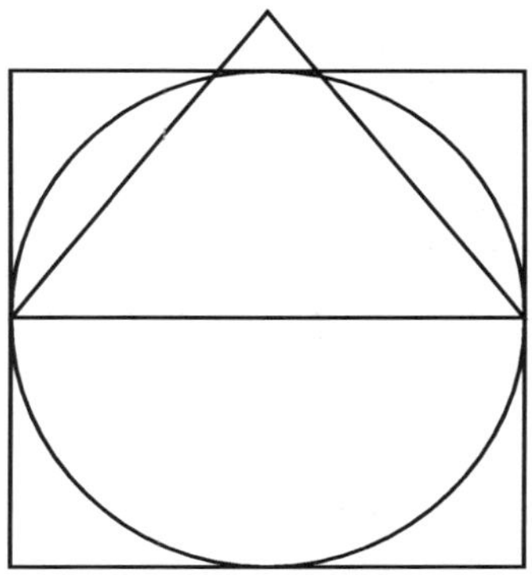

Let us take this newly created 51.83 degree triangle and place it directly in the center of an equal circle and square. You can see that the top of this triangle sticks out the top slightly.

Now lets add another circle that will encompass the top of the 51.83 degree triangle, and create another smaller circle that intersects the diameter of square and circle.

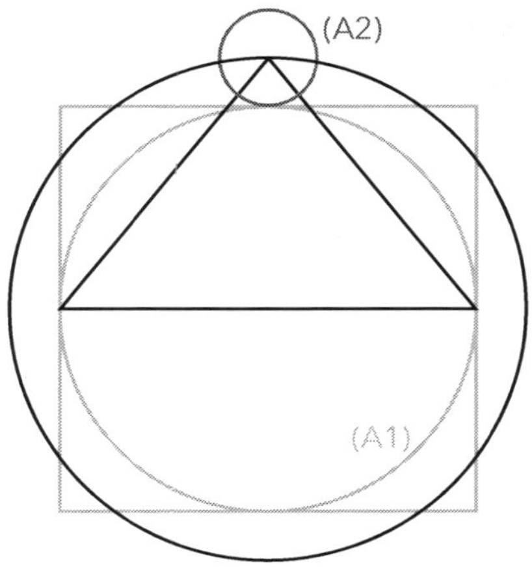

This image was how the ancient geometers represented the creation of our physical Earth and Moon. That the ratios of this design perfectly matched the ratios of our Earth (A1) and Moon (A2). It was the relationship of the triangle that held them. This is the same relationship between spirit and matter.

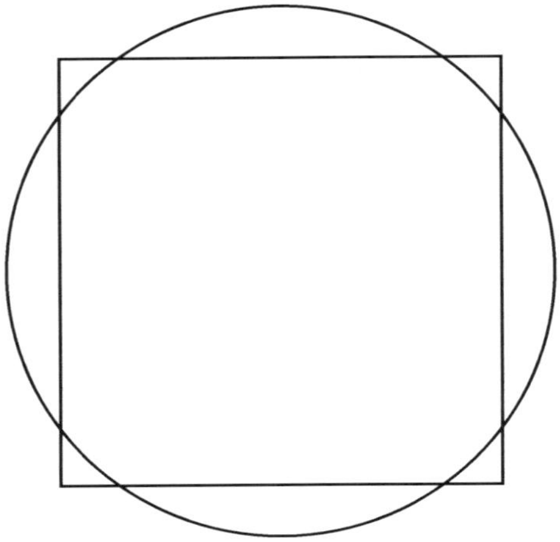

Creating the 'Squared Circle"

When you take out the triangle, the inner circle and the smaller circle. You are left with a perfect squared circle. This is where you get the term *"Squaring the Circle".*

This term was used in varying contexts but for our purposes we will define this as "bridging spirit with matter in perfect harmony". This was the goal of the ancient mystics, geometers and alchemists. They were trying to bridge matter and spirit for the goal of transformation. Turning lead to gold, matter to spirit, dull to enlightened. They would visually show this as either a triangle with its capstone. The capstone was defined by the intersecting line of the square and the circle through the triangle.

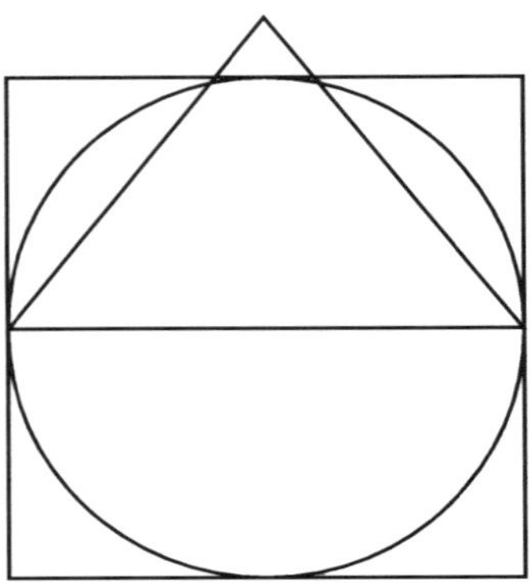

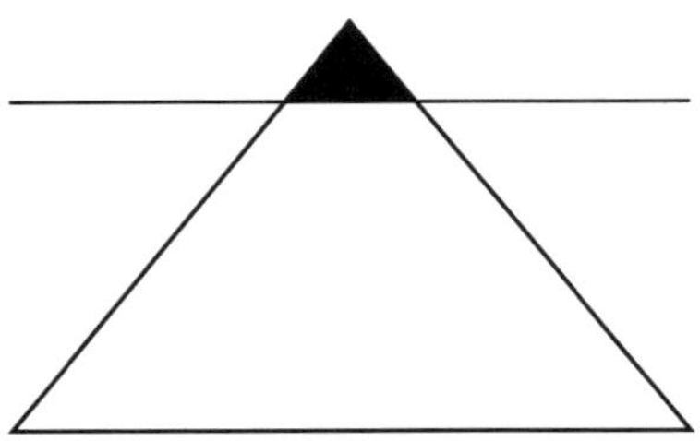

Defining the capstone

The capstone on the back of the U
Dollar follows a different geomet

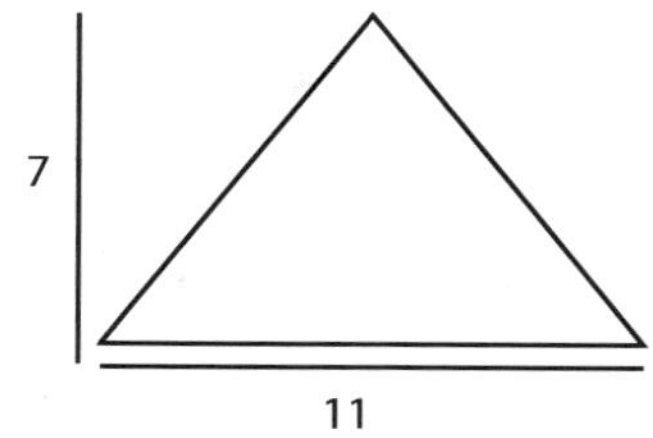

Pyramid Harmonics:

If we scale down the 51.83 degree pyramid you get the ratio 11 by 7.
If we divide 11 by 7 we get 1.571. This is exactly half of pi 3.1415.

If we take these numbers and start to 'play' with them, we start to discover some very interesting patterns. For example if we that the numbers 1 through 7 and multiply them we get the number 5040. This was Plato's 'Magic' number.

1x2x3x4x5x6x7 = 5040

If we continue this pattern and now finish the sequence by multiplying the remaining numbers 8 through 11 we get another interesting pattern.

8x9x10x11 = 7920

The Earths diameter is calculated at approximately 7,920 miles.

When we play with these numbers more we start to get some other very important numbers.

7920 / 5040 = 1.571 (half of pi)
7920 + 5040 = 12960 (half of the precession of the zodiac - 25920 years)
7920 - 5040 = 2880 (harmonic of light)

The number Pi (3.141), denoted by the Greek letter π - is one of the most common constants in all of mathematics. It is the circumference of any circle, divided by its diameter. Nobody knows its exact value, because no matter how many digits you calculate it to, the number never ends. This makes Pi a transcendental number which goes on infinity.

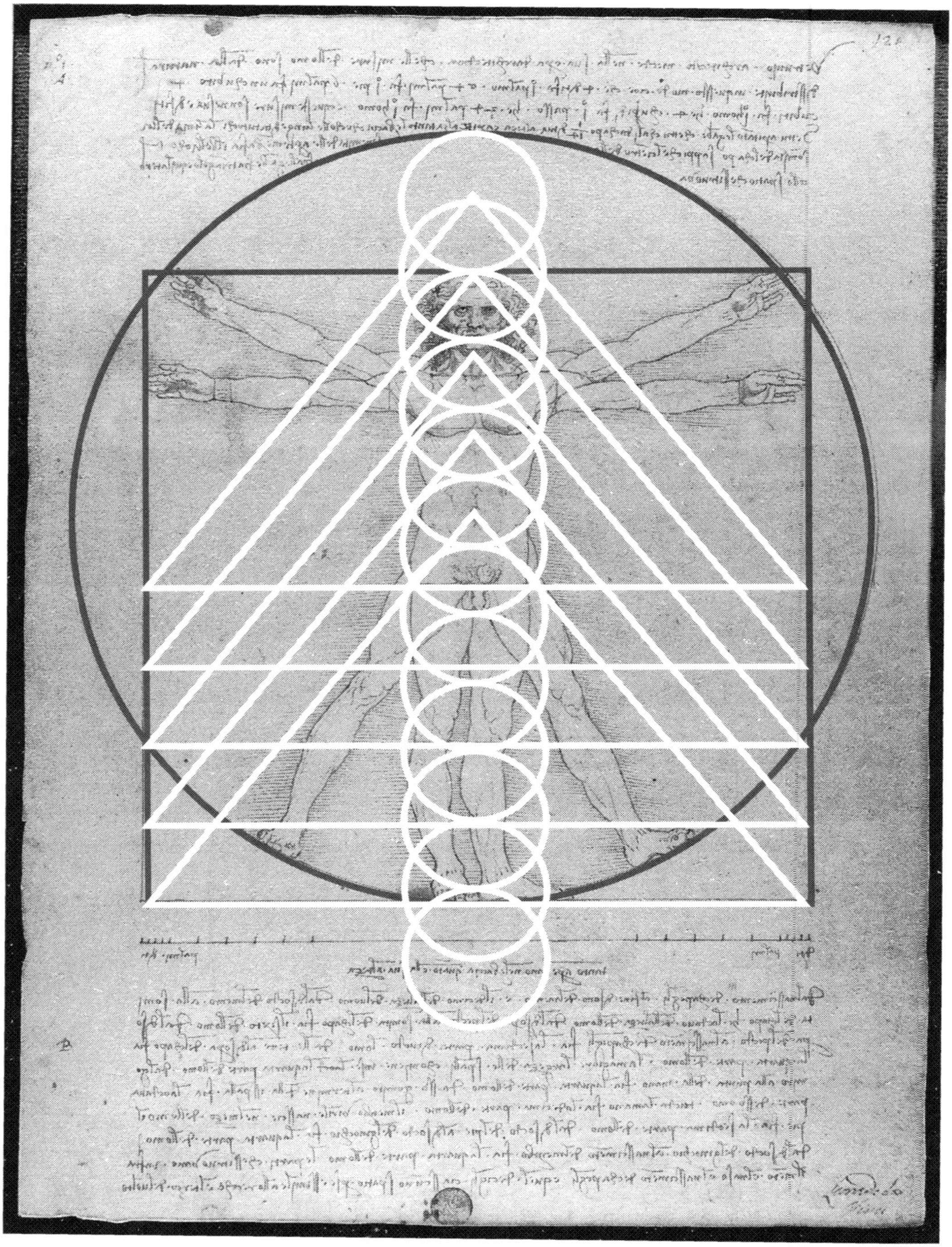

Da Vinci's Code - Vitruvian Man

Here we have the famous artwork of Leonardo Da Vinci, where he demonstrates the perfect ratios of the human form within a square and a circle. If we add the 51.83 triangle we can see how he figured out these proportions of the human body quite easily. Not only does this art show the direct link between sacred geometry and the ratios of the human body, but it also shows how the human form is a direct reflection of the ratios of the earth, moon and creation itself.

Once we understand the basic order and function of sacred geometry, we can then start to see the great mysteries of creation unravel itself before our eyes. Remember, Da Vinci was supposedly a grand master of the Mason's, which would mean he had great knowledge in very well kept secrets. As we can see from this artwork he new all about these ratios and the divine design of creation.

The Dimensions of Time & Space

Throughout history shamans, mystics, alchemists, and spiritual people from around the world have always made it a point to connect and call in the 7 directions before any spiritual practice. They would connect to the earth, the sky, the four directions and the center within them. By connecting to each one of these fields they are consciously anchoring and centering themselves within the spheres of time and space. This connects them to the natural fields of energy around them and expands their consciousness out to receive new energies.

If you were to graphically show this connection, you would have to draw 6 circles around 1 center circle. This creates what geometers call the seed of life, which is one of the oldest and most mystical symbols.

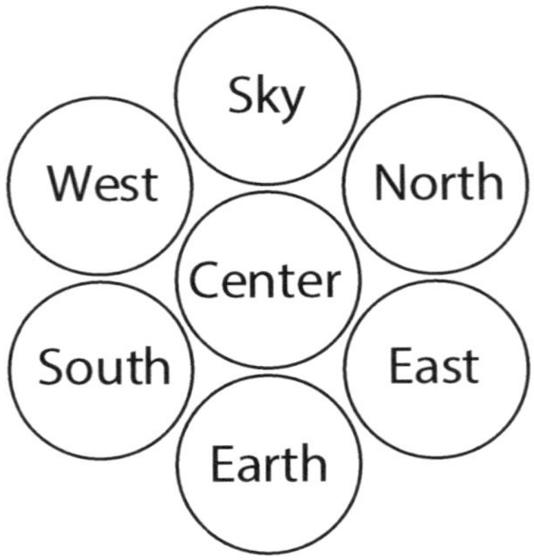

The 7 circles that represent the directions of 3 dimensional space

When we bring the six outer circles into the seventh inner circle we create the symbol of the 'Seed Of Life'

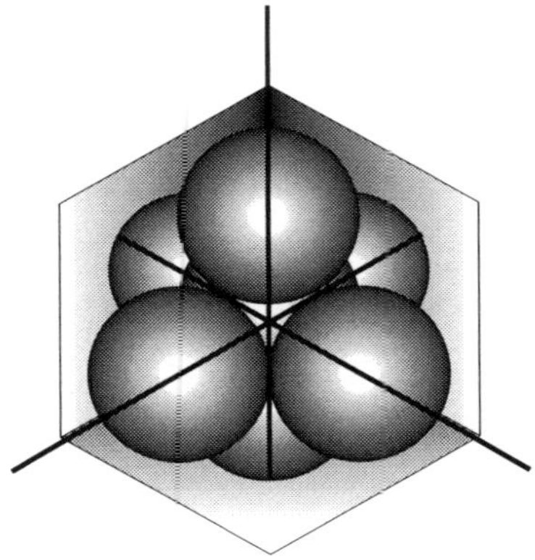

3D representation of the 'Seed Of Life'

Picture the third dimensional world. You have the Earth below you, the sky above and the four directions around you. Most importantly you have your inner world, we can refer to this as our center or heart.

When creating sacred space, people from many different traditions call in the 'Directions'. When we practice this act, we are consciously bringing these fields into our awareness and anchoring them within our center. We can then picture this as the symbol of the 'Seed Of Life'. Which shows the six directional fields being brought into the center circle.

We can also take the 'Seed Of Life' and visualize it in its 3 Dimensional form (pictured above). If you can imagine your first day of life after conception. Your first cells begin to divide to create the blueprint of your physical form. On the day 2 of life you would take the formation of the 'Seed Of Life'.

If we use the 'Seed Of Life' and continue to expand this formation, the next image we will create is what is know as 'The Flower Of Life'. This symbol is very ancient. There is an example of this symbol etched into the Temple of Osiris, Egypt. It is estimated that this example is over 8,000 years old.

The 'Flower Of Life'

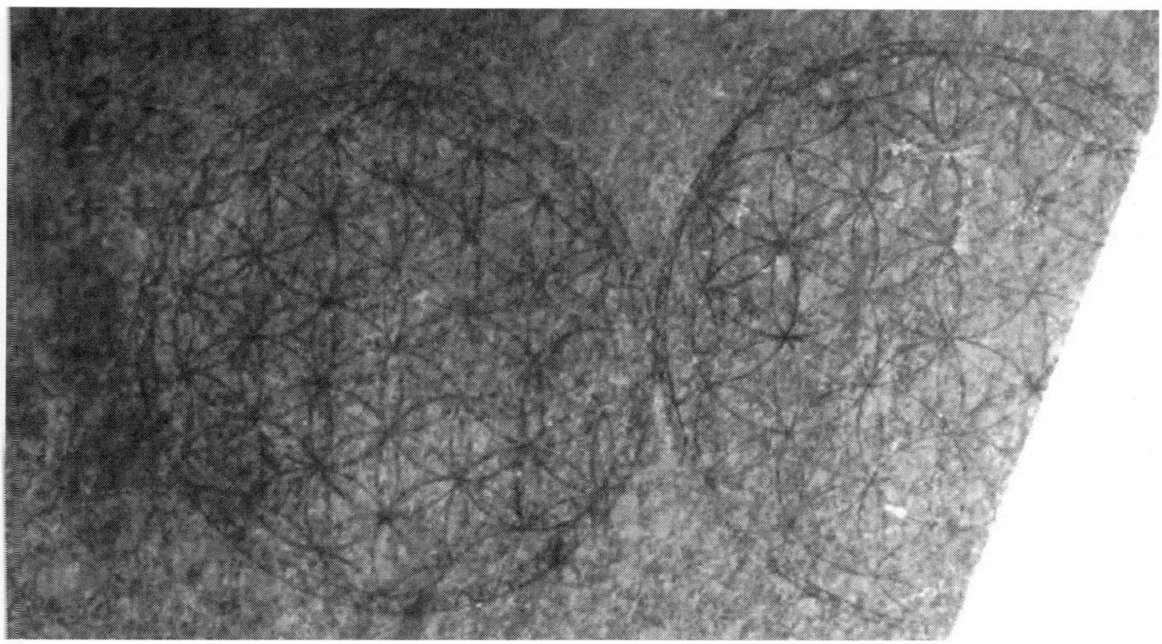

The 'Flower Of Life' etched into the wall at
the Temple of Osiris, Egypt.

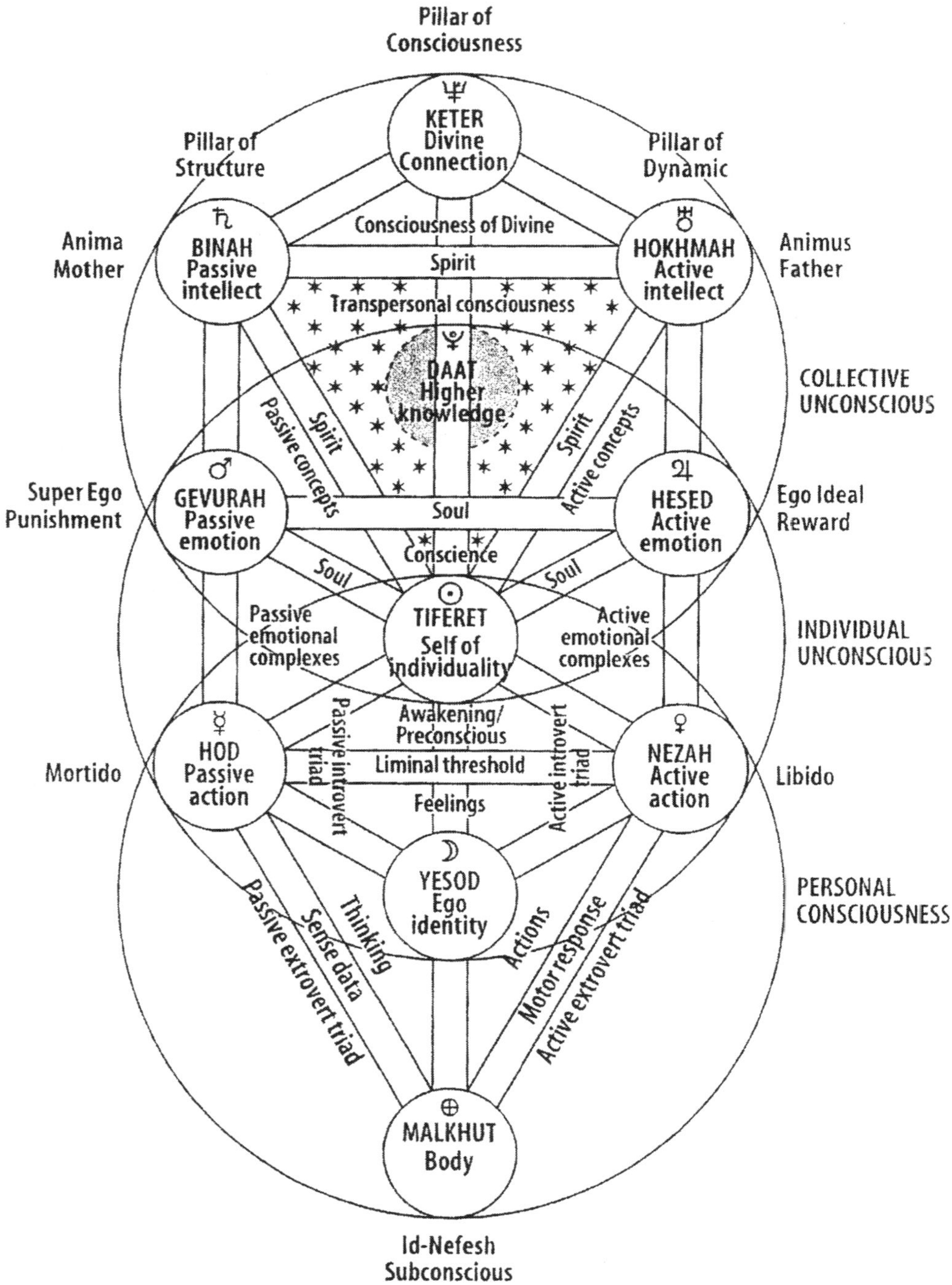

Pillar of Consciousness
Pillar of Structure
Pillar of Dynamic
KETER
Divine Connection
Anima
Mother
BINAH
Passive intellect
HOKHMAH
Active intellect
Animus
Father
Consciousness of Divine
Spirit
Transpersonal consciousness
DAAT
Higher knowledge
COLLECTIVE UNCONSCIOUS
Passive concepts
Spirit
Spirit
Active concepts
Super Ego
Punishment
GEVURAH
Passive emotion
Soul
HESED
Active emotion
Ego Ideal
Reward
Conscience
Soul
Soul
Passive emotional complexes
TIFERET
Self of individuality
Active emotional complexes
INDIVIDUAL UNCONSCIOUS
Passive introvert triad
Awakening/ Preconscious
Liminal threshold
Feelings
Active introvert triad
Mortido
HOD
Passive action
NEZAH
Active action
Libido
YESOD
Ego identity
PERSONAL CONSCIOUSNESS
Passive extrovert triad
Sense data
Thinking
Actions
Motor response
Active extrovert triad
MALKHUT
Body
Id-Nefesh
Subconscious

The Tree of Life Code

The Tree of Life is a mystical symbol used in the Kabbalah of esoteric Judaism to describe the path to God and the manner in which the world was created. The Kabbalists developed this concept into a full model of reality, using the tree to depict a map of Creation. Kabbalists believe the Tree of Life to be a diagrammatic representation of the process by which the Universe came into being.

Tree of Life placed on The Flower Of Life

When the Tree of Life is multiplied and rotated 6 times

Creating the geometry of Metatrons Cube

As you can see the Tree of Life fits perfectly in the flower of life formation. If we take the tree of life and rotate it 6 times we get an interesting geometry. This symbol is known as 'Metatrons Cube'. This geometry represents the blueprint in which we can create the 5 platonic solids.

The Platonic solids represent the five building blocks of creation. Their names are derived from the number of their faces: 4, 6, 8,12, and 20.

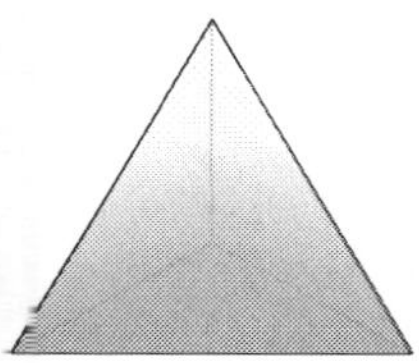

tetrahedron (fire)

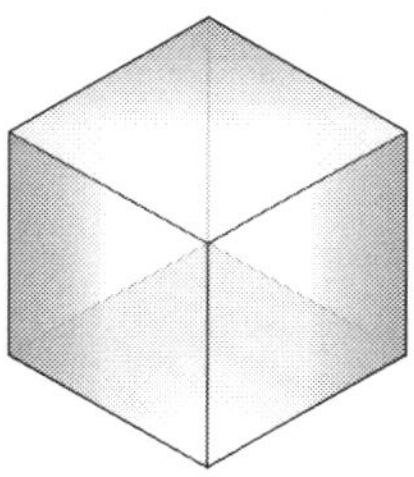

cube (earth)

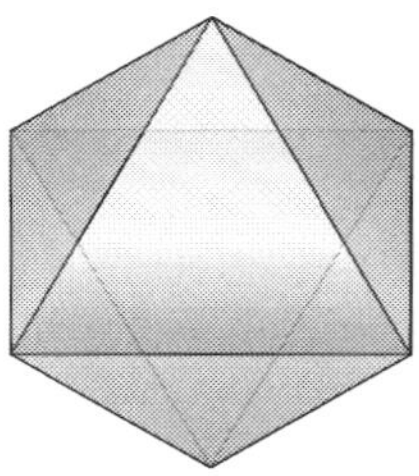

octahedron (air)

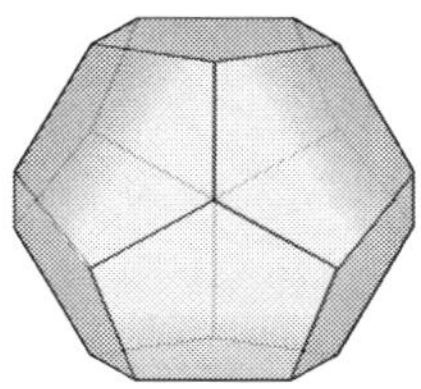

dodecahedron (ether)

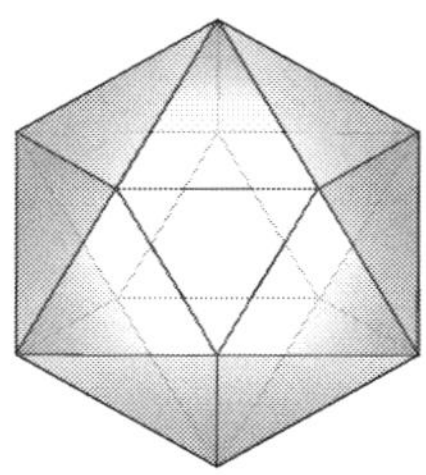

icosahedron (water)

The Universal Grid

If we take the flower of life and draw lines through all its points, we get a grid pattern. There is a natural grid system of our planet that follows this exact pattern. It is called the Hartmann and Curry grid. The Curry grid runs diagonally to the poles, east to west at 3 meters apart; Hartmann lines run both east-west and north - south forming a grid across the Earth's surface with a distance of 2 meters in the north - south direction and 2.5 meters in the east - west direction.

Not only is this grid present on the planet, but it also applies to our physical bodies, chakras, meridians and energetic bodies. This pattern branches out to our solar system, galaxy and universe. This is the blueprint in which all consciousness and form manifest. It is amazing to think that this knowledge has been with us for more then eight thousand years. Which brings up another question, how did we have such advanced knowledge when mankind was supposedly living in caves?

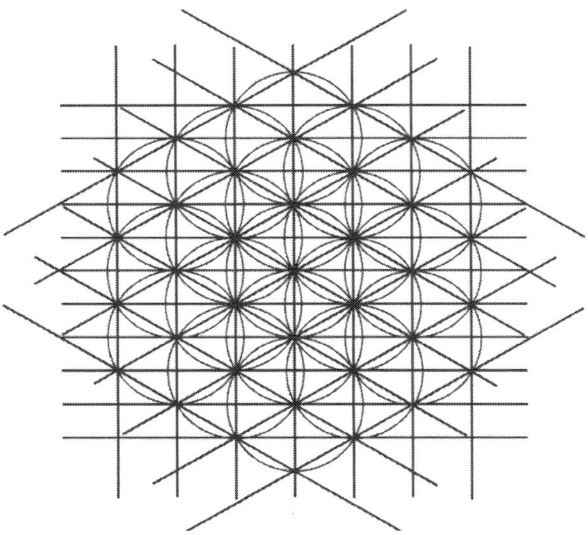

The Hartmann & Curry grid follow the same geometry as the Flower of Life grid

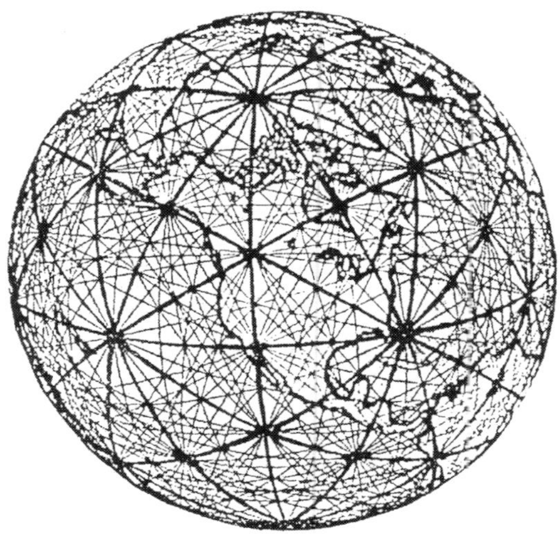

The Russian Earth grid which supposedly depicts the energy lines of the planet

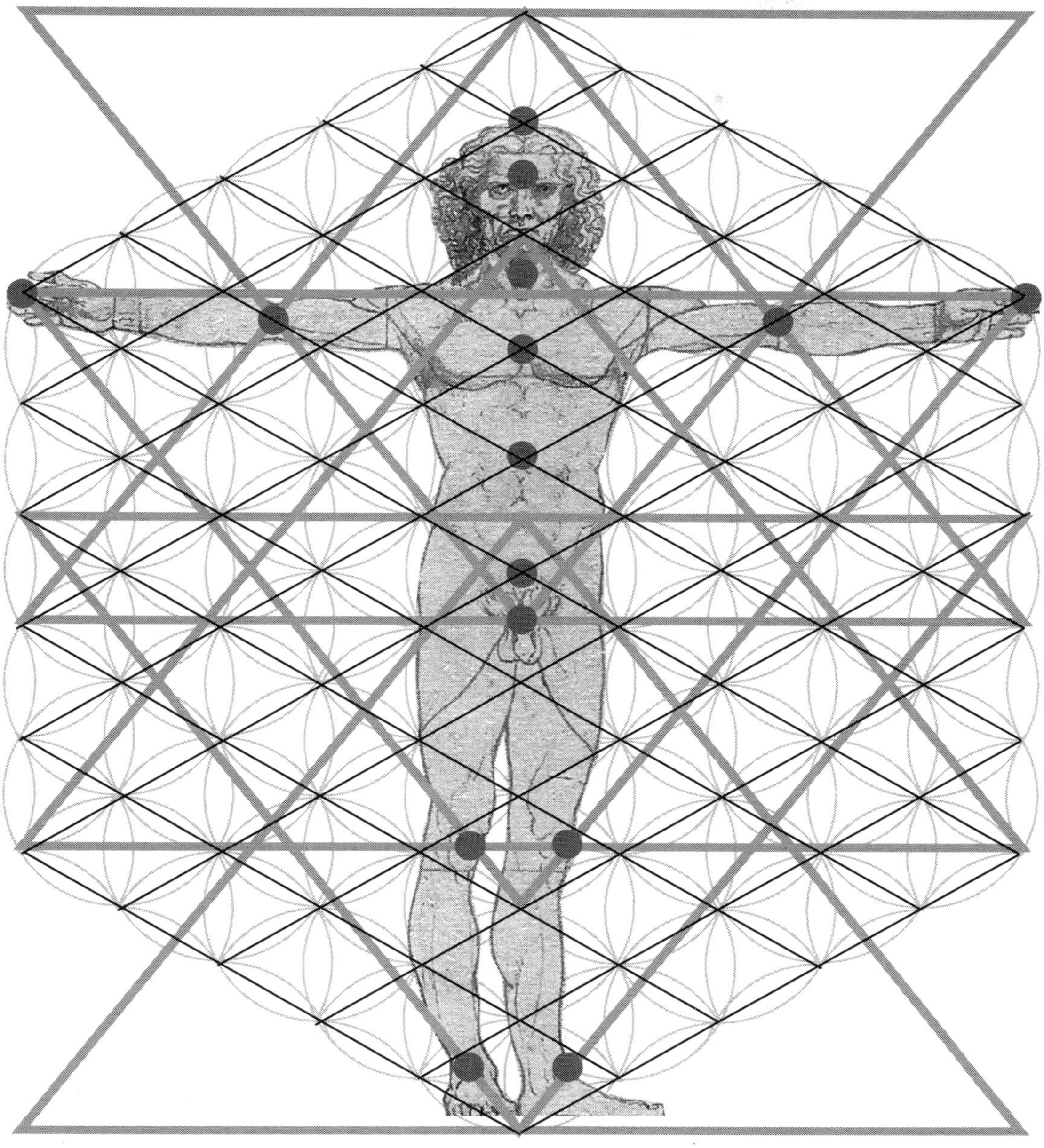

Sacred Geometry of the Human body

Sacred Geometry of the Body

Here is the human body laid out on the Flower of Life with the 51.83 degree triangles. You can see that the layout of the chakra system corresponds to the sacred design of all of these elements combined.

Look at how similar the layout of these triangles are to the Sri Yantra Mandala of Hinduism.

Sacred Geometry of the Human body

The Sri Yantra is the Mandala which symbolizes the physical universe and its unmanifest source.

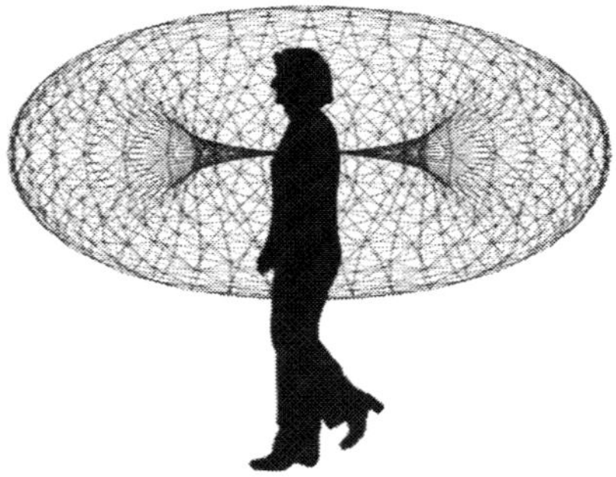

Visualization a chakra field

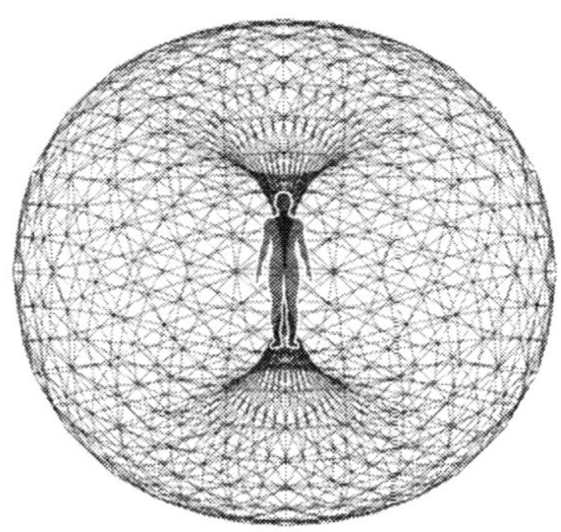

Visualization of energy body

Cymatics - The geometry of sound

Cymatics is the study of the geometric pattens produced by sound frequencies. This is achieved through the medium of sand, water, or oil to created these amazing geometric designs.

This shows the direct connection between frequency (consciousness) and geometry. As you can clearly see these geometries follow the same order as the flower of life pattern.

When we say sacred mantras or tone certain sounds we are going to resonance with specific geometries of consciousness. This by itself is a very powerful healing and meditation system, because we are using our own voice or mental thought forms to go into resonance and connect with specific vibrational natures of creation itself.

Vortex Geometry

Pictured above is another amazing example of cymatics. This geometry shows the absolute perfection of a mathematical vortex structure. We can reproduce the exact same geometry by taking the 'Seed Of Life' and rotating it on its axis.

We can find the same geometry throughout the natural world. The most obvious examples we can see come from the plant kingdom.

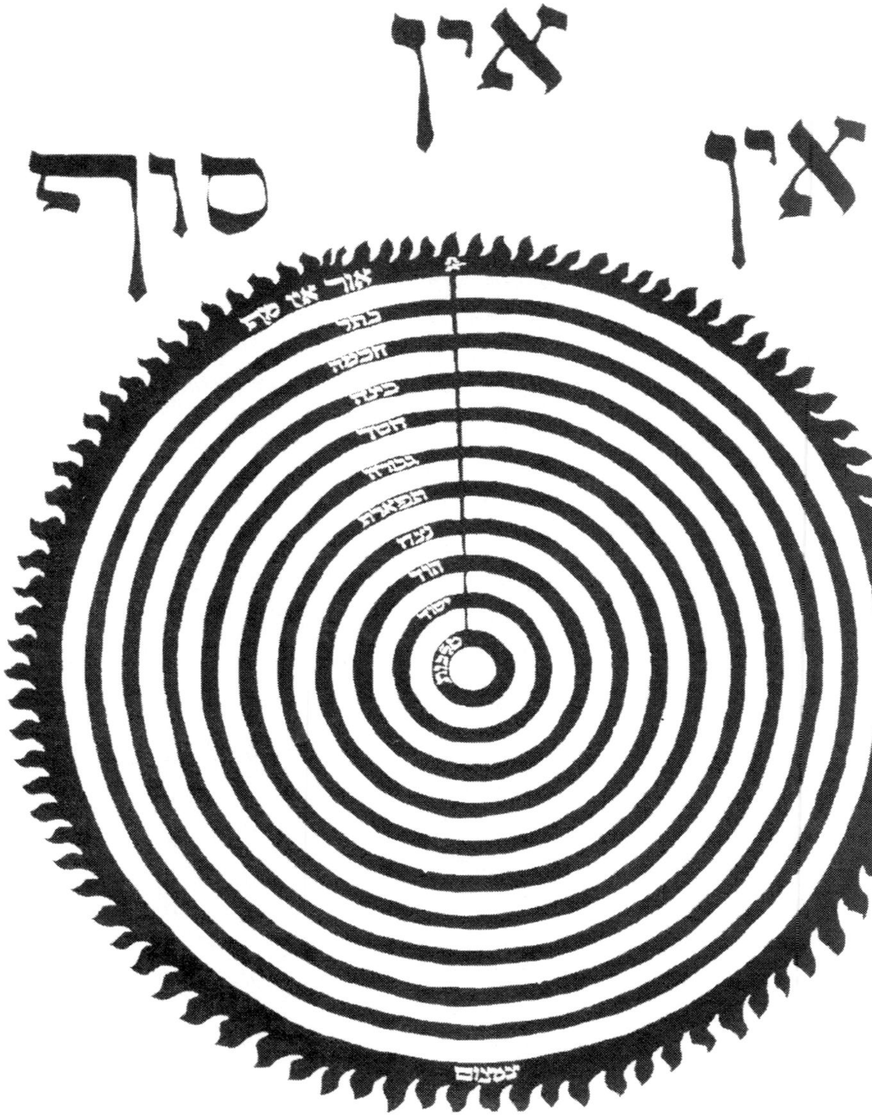

Ein Sof Mandala

Ein Sof - Mandala of Infinite Light In Kabbalah, Ein Sof is understood as God before manifestation. Ein Sof may be translated as unending or Infinite. This would be meditated on while saying the mantra “Ein Sof” or “Ein Sof Ein”. When meditating on this Mandala you will start to see rainbows of color emanating from the consecutive circles.

The Yosef Codes

Root Chakra

Mantra: TA TEY

Mandala Intention:

The Root Chakra is located at the base of spine. This chakra is responsible for connecting and grounding us to the Earths energetic fields. Which strengthens our physical nature and enhances our connection to mother Earth.

This code may assist mental imbalances by grounding our energies into the Earths grid. This action helps bring balance to the physical and mental bodies.

Recommendations:

Plant this code at the base of tree or place on the foundation of a house to ground and enhance the connection to mother earths energy fields.

Meditating on this code may assist in getting to the root of a problem.

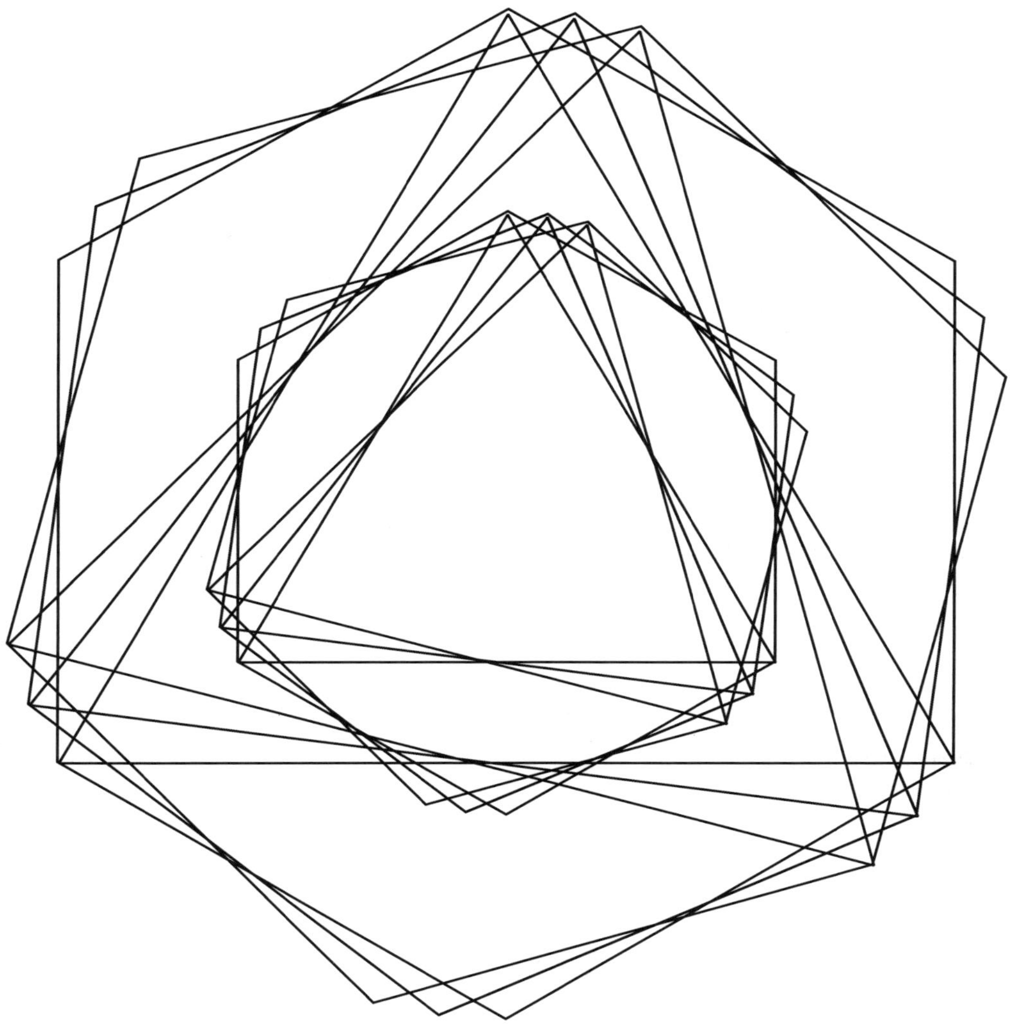

Sacral Chakra

Mantra: TEE LA SO DA

Mandala Intention:

Located just below the navel, this chakra connects to our sexual and creative nature. This is where our fire for life is located.

This code can be used to enhances musical ability, dance movements, and composition.

Fans the inner fire to assist those whom are recovering from an illness, by stimulating the flow of energies to moving again.

Recommendations:

Place this code on the Sacral Chakra to increase sexual desire, strength and increases energy flow.

Beneficial to place this code in recording rooms, dance studios and music spaces to enhance the natural flow of sound and rhythm.

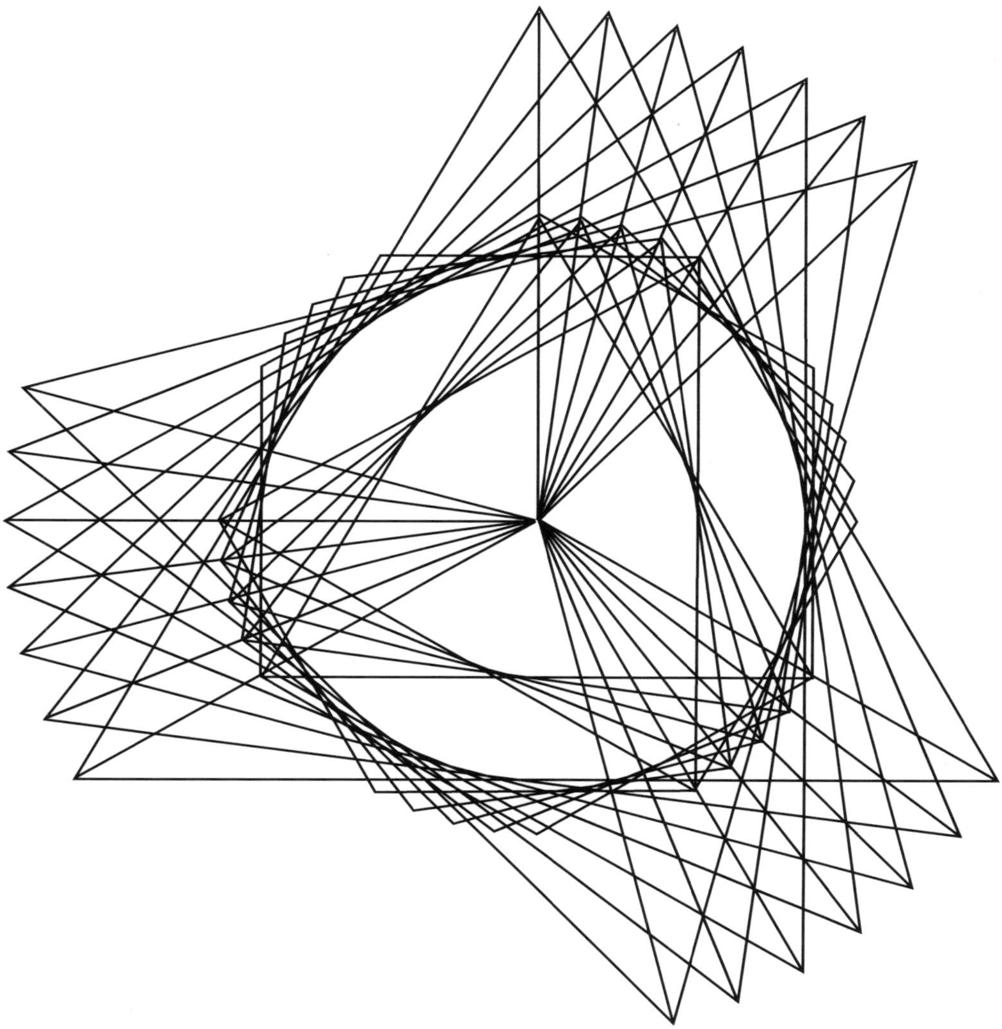

Solar Chakra

Mantra: TEE DOH LA

Mandala Intention:

Located at your solar plexus, this chakra connects us to our power. The solar plexus is also the place where we can store and build healing energy in the body.

This code enhances breathing, telepathy, sending messages and assists in shamanic traveling.

Recommendations:

Meditate on this code before public speaking or decision making.

Place on solar chakra to assist in breathing and to help bring power back to the energetic system.

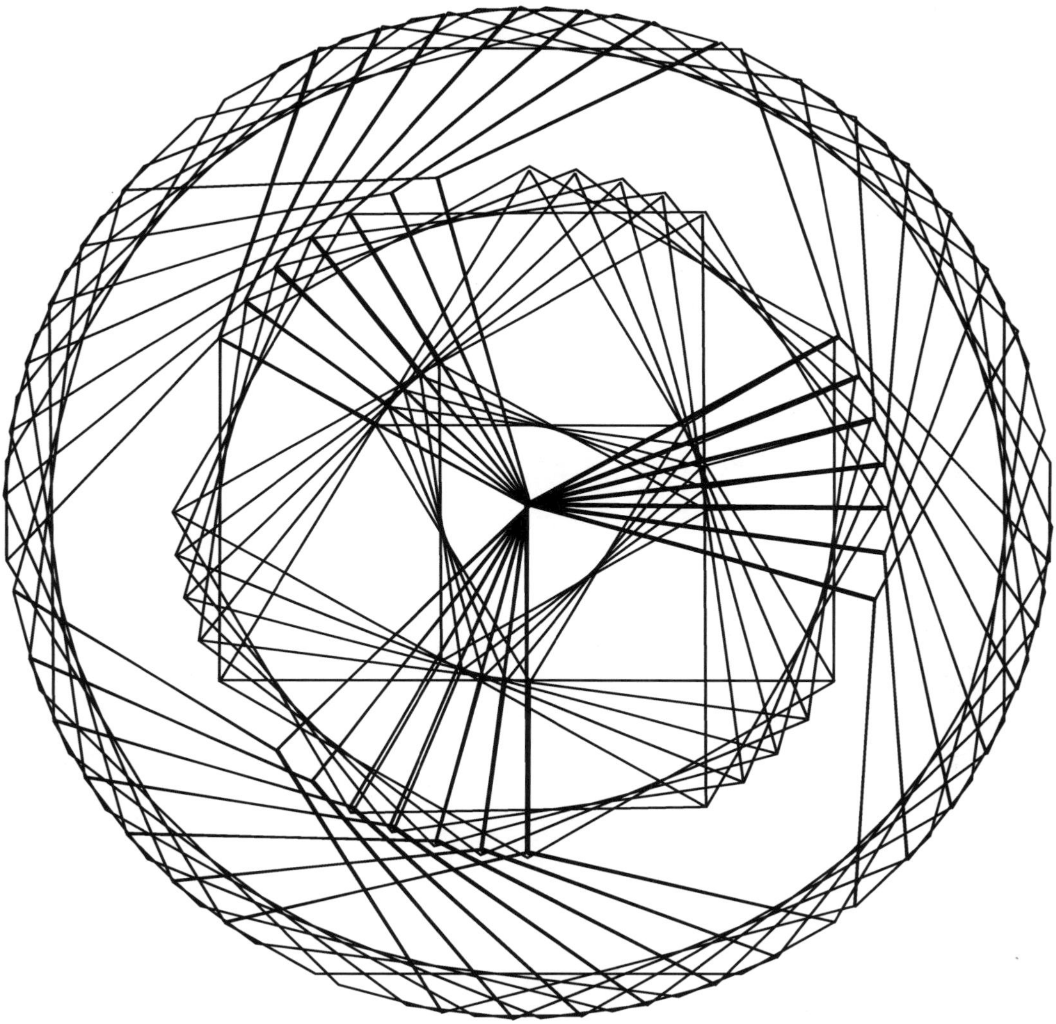

Heart Chakra

Mantra: DOH ME SO DOH

Mandala Intention:

Located at your heart center, this chakra connects us to our divine self. The heart is also our connection to universe within us and outside of us.

This code enhances meditation practices and connects us to the energies of the universal mother.

The energies of this code is also beneficial for working with the circulation of the hands and feet.

Beneficial to send this energy to large bodies of water to assist in purification.

Recommendations:

Place on heart chakra to enhance your connection with the universal mother to bring in and connect to the energies of love for healing.

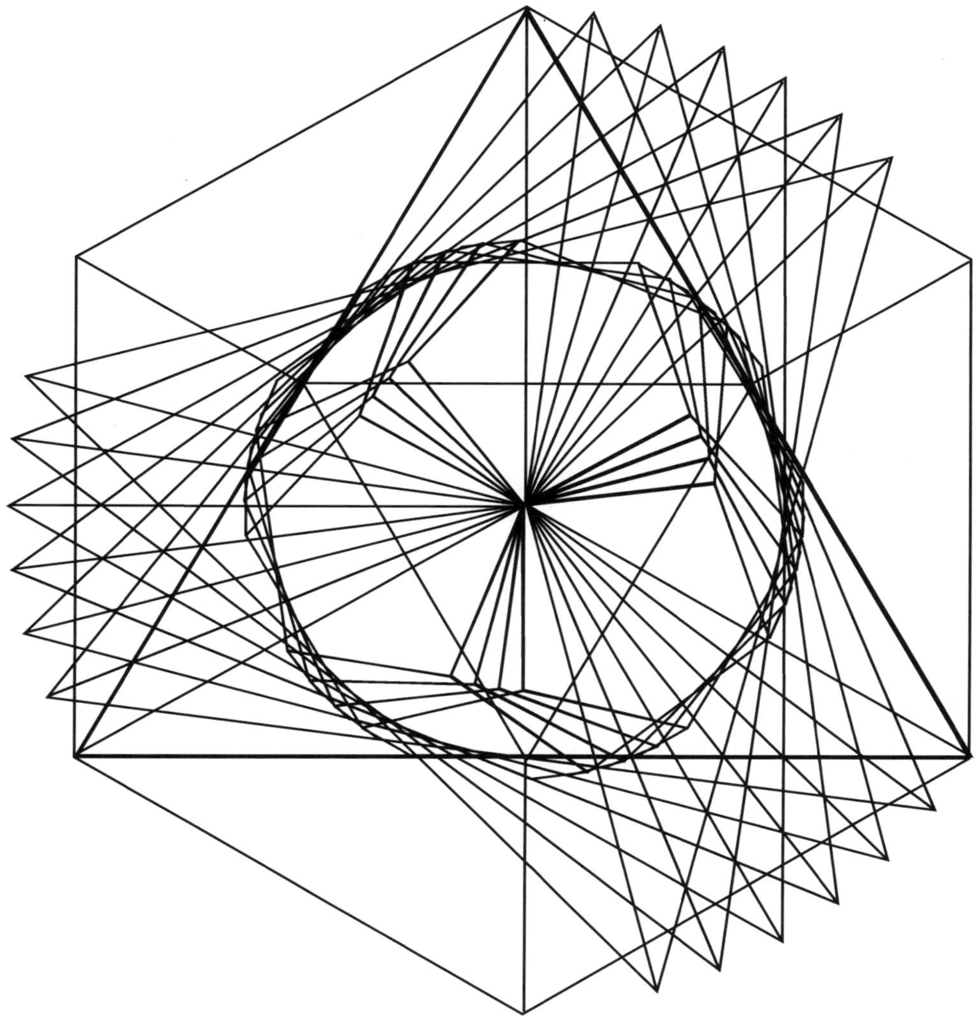

Throat Chakra

Mantra: TAY TAY LA LA ME

Mandala Intention:

Located at the center of your throat, this chakra enhances communication and expression of who we are.

This code is beneficial for working with throat issues, singing and public speaking.

Helps channelers and psychics enhance their connection to higher spirit guides for communication.

Recommendations:

Place on throat chakra before giving an important speech so that all messages will be properly expressed and received.

Use before and after singing to assist in bringing the energies of the throat back into balance.

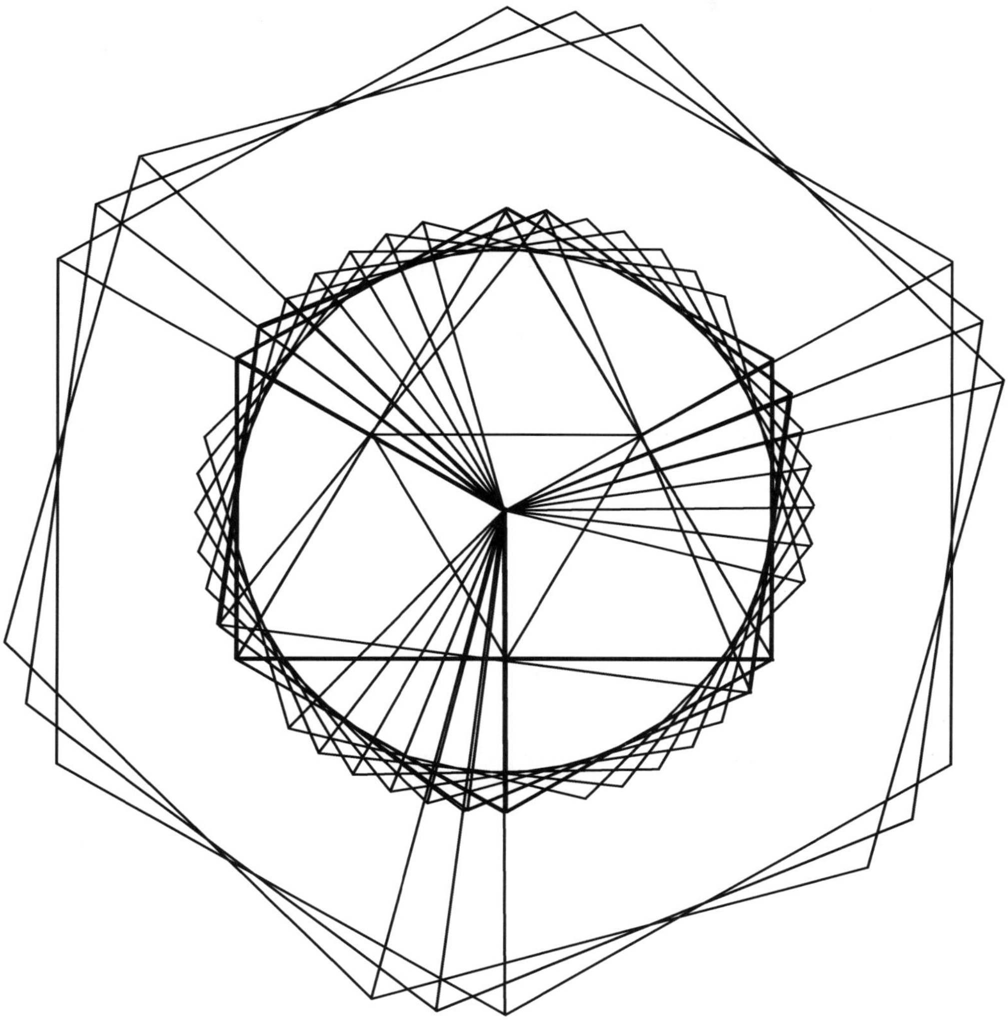

Third Eye Chakra

Mantra: TEE TEE LA LA SO DOH ME

Mandala Intention:

Located at the center of your forehead, this chakra enhances inner vision and intuition.

This code is beneficial for remote viewing, soul retrievals and shamanic journeying.

The energies of this code may be used for dementia, alzheimer's and brain injuries at their early stages.

Recommendations:

Place on third eye chakra to enhance inner visions, intuition, remote viewing and any other journey states for healing.

Meditating on this code will assist in healing and bringing clarity back to the mental body.

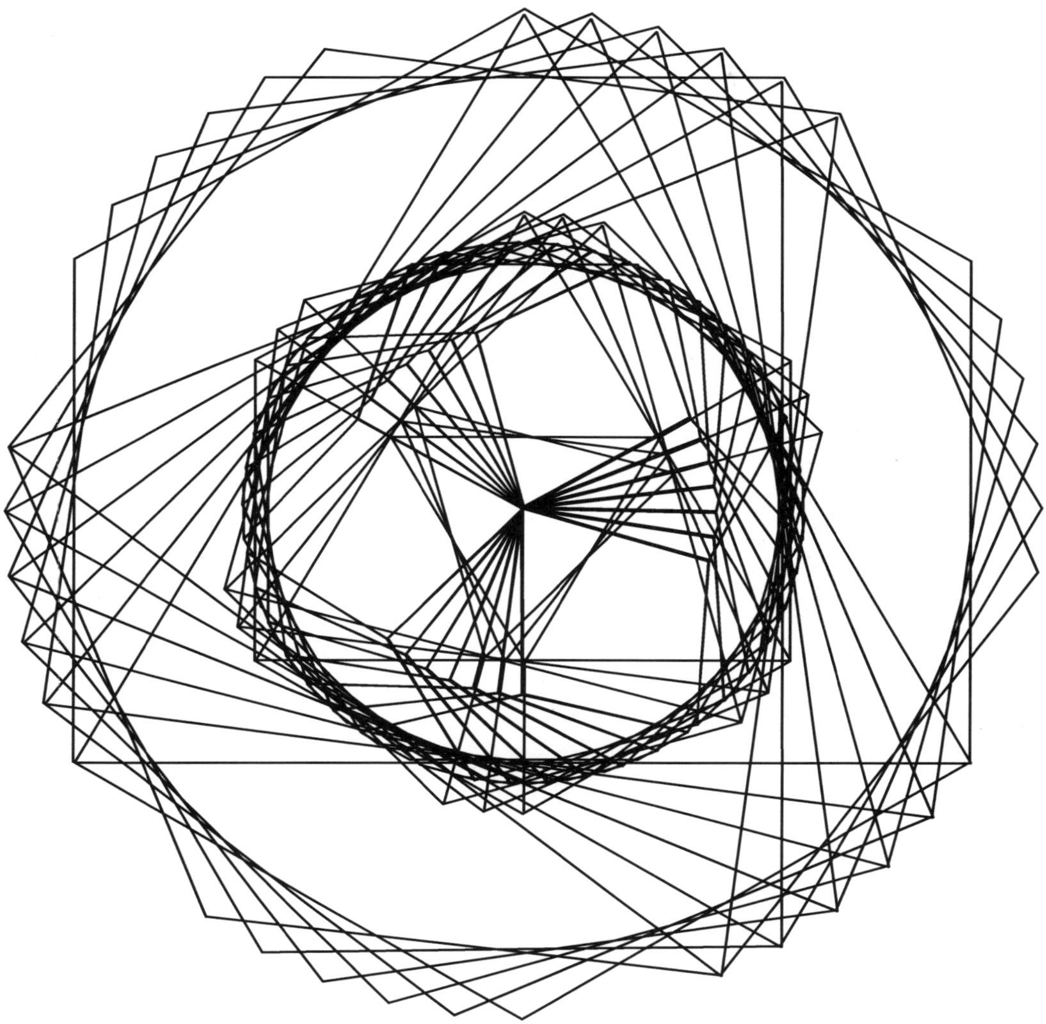

Crown Chakra

Mantra: TA LA LE LOW HO

Mandala Intention:

Located at the top of your head, this chakra connects us to our source.

This code is beneficial for inter-dimensional travels.

Assists in purifying and energetically changes the vibration of water.

Assists us seeing hidden messages.

Recommendations:

Place on mirrors, churches, temples and healing rooms to create sacred space.

Meditating on this code will assist in connecting us to our higher self.

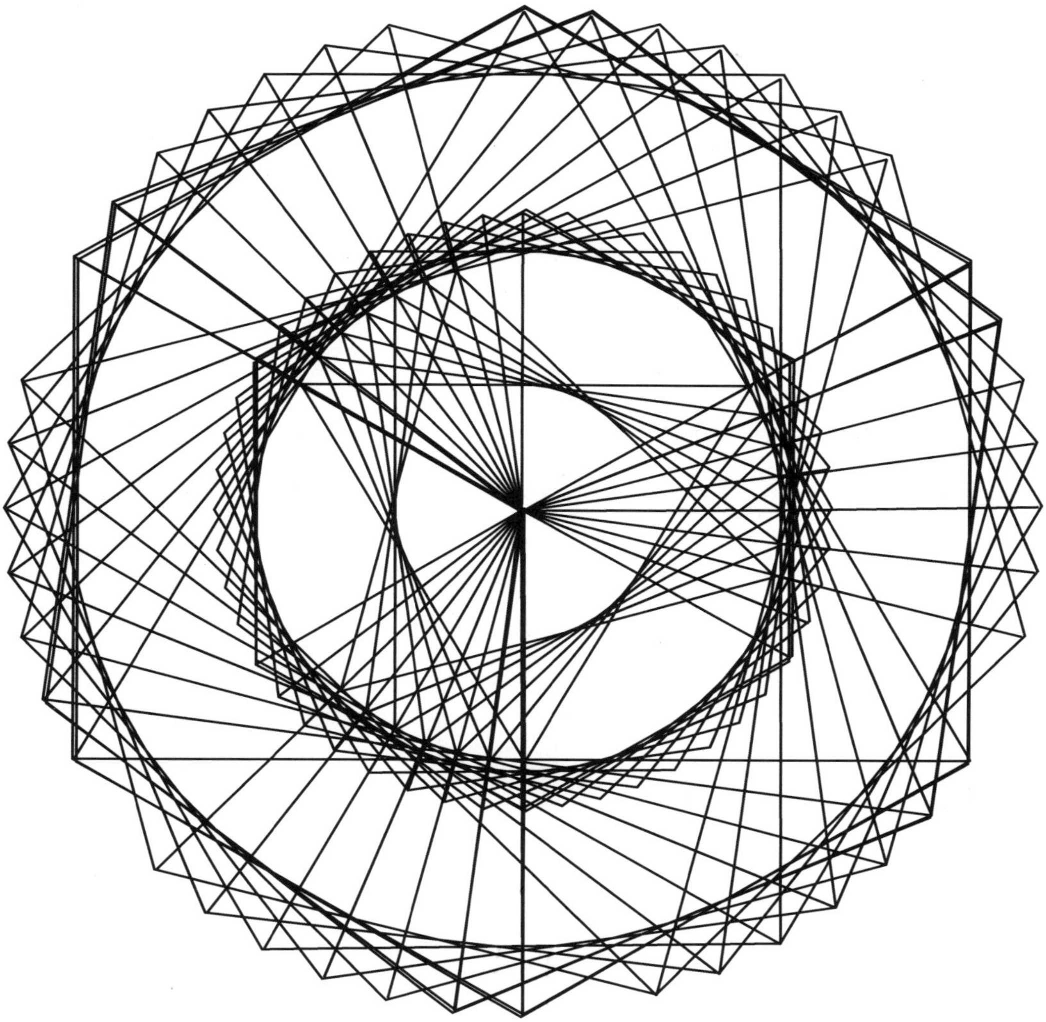

Higher Crown Chakra

Mantra: TA LA LA TAY ME

Mandala Intention:

Located above your head, this chakra connects us with ancestral spirits and guides.

This code assists in exorcisms and taking earth bound spirits to the light.

Recommendations:

Can be placed on objects and chakras that need clearing.

Place in bedrooms and the areas that pets sleep in.

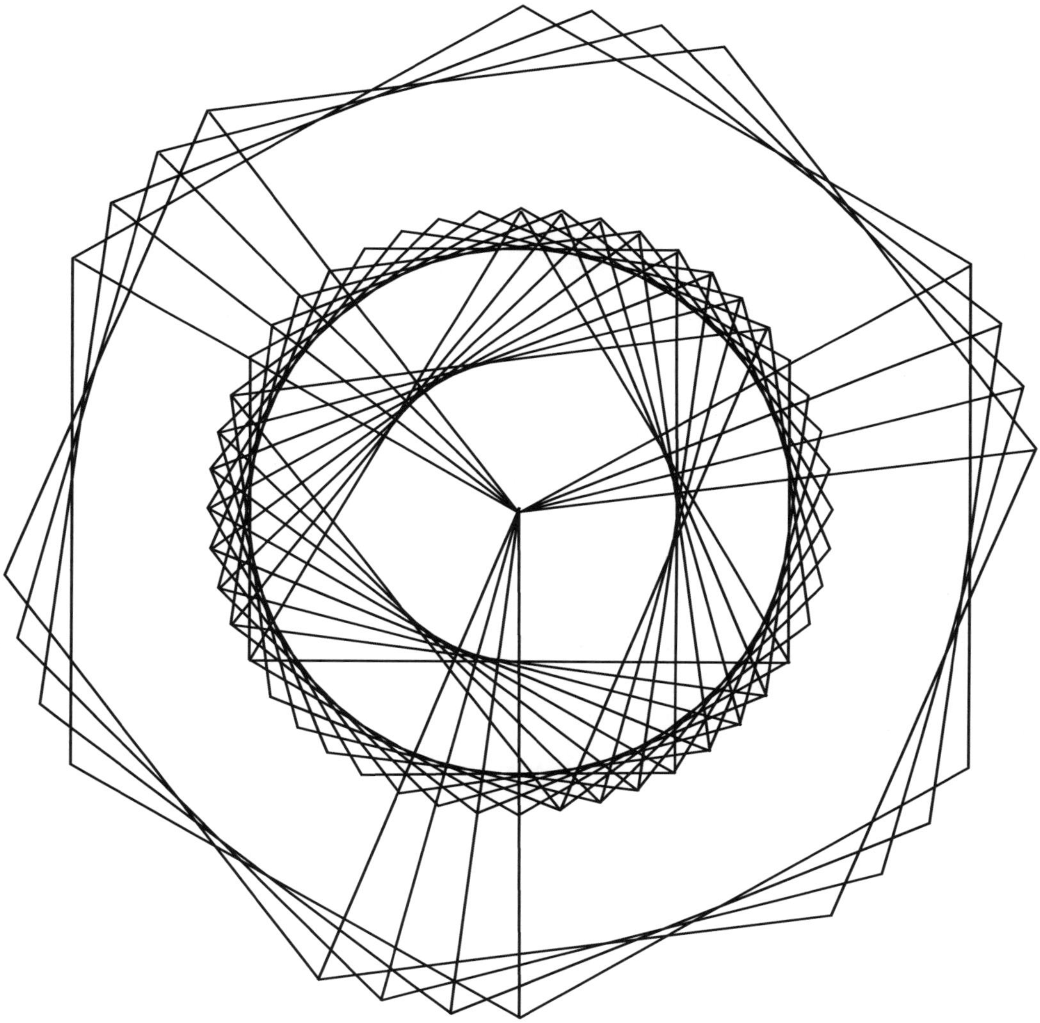

Chakra Alignment

Mantra: DOH ME SO DOH DOHHH

Mandala Intention:
Balances and aligns all chakras and chakra systems.

Recommendations:
Great for putting on native rattles and massage tables.

Place inside cars and planes.

Beneficial for athletes.

Meditating on these energies or carrying this code will assist in energetically balancing and aligning the chakras.

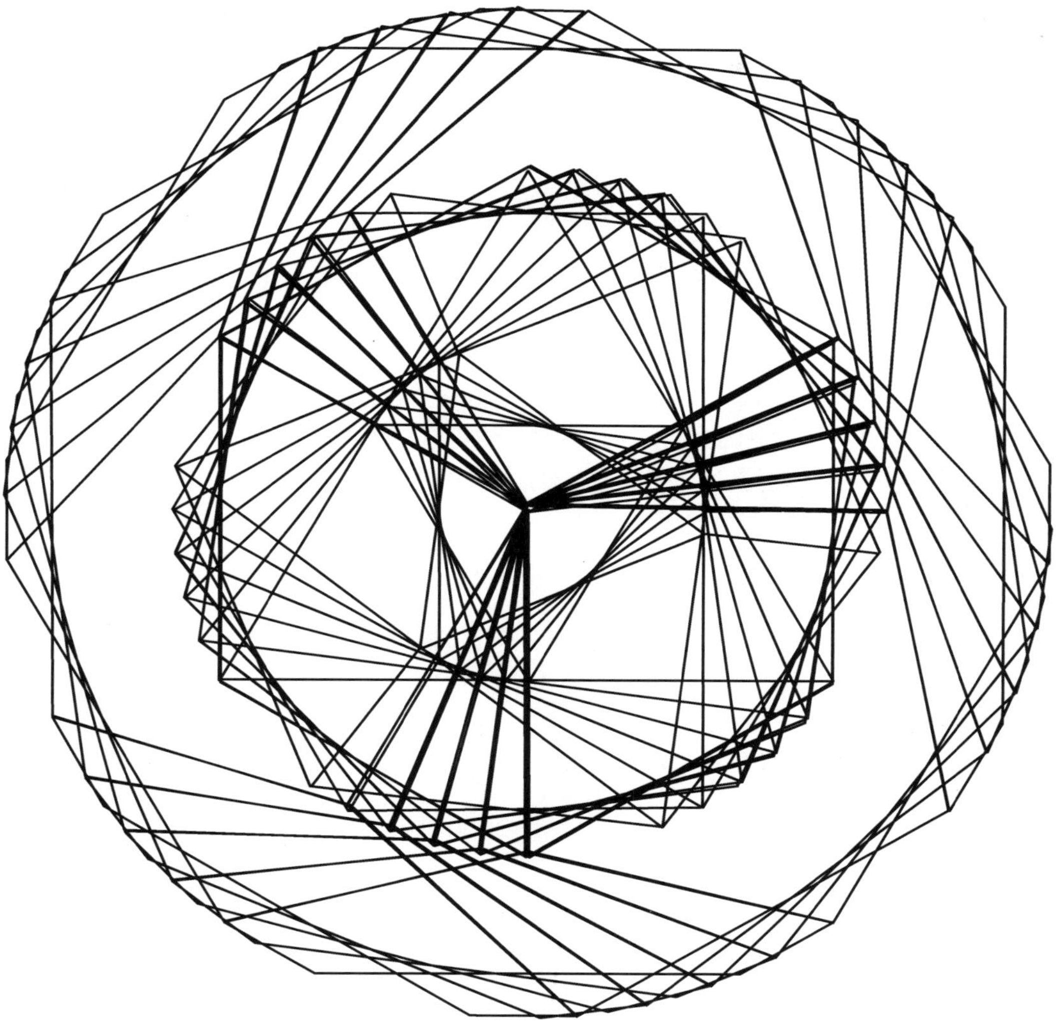

Elemental Balance

Mantra: DOE RAY ME SO SEE

Mandala Intention:

Balances all the elements. (Earth, Air, Fire, Water, Ether.)

Beneficial for gardens and parks, this code harmonizes all earth divas, guardians and earth energies.

This code can be used as a general balancer of energies.

Recommendations:

Place code in gardens, parks, and crops.

Meditating on this code assists in balancing the elemental energies of the body.

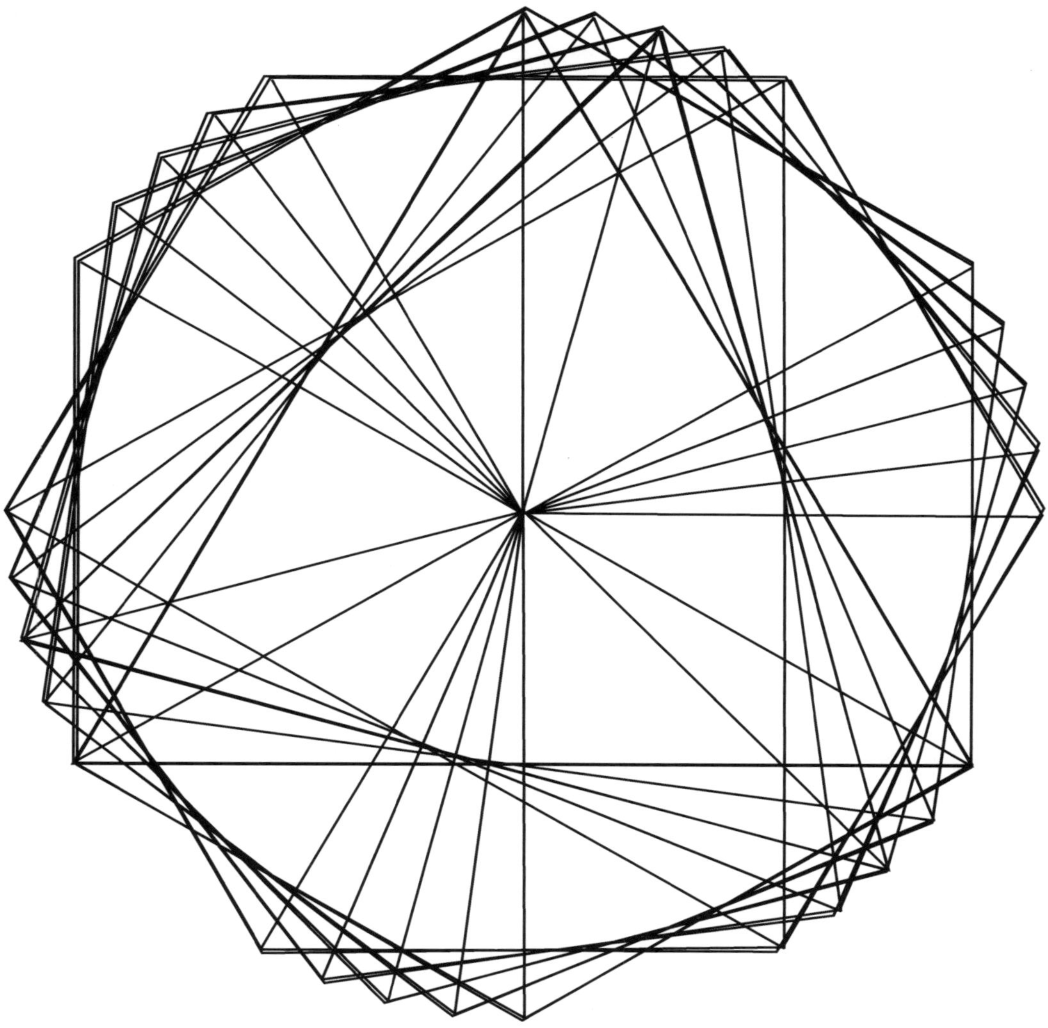

4 Body Alignment

Mantra: TEE LA TEE LA

Mandala Intention:

The energy of this code enhances our senses. Our sight, hearing, taste, smell and touch.

Assists the energetic bodies in communicating and working together as one.

Can be used by healers to help tune into more intuitive information about their clients healing needs.

Recommendations:

Run the energy of the code over chakras to enhance and align the connections between the energetic bodies. (Physical, Emotional, Mental and Etheric.)

Beneficial to be placed in healing rooms.

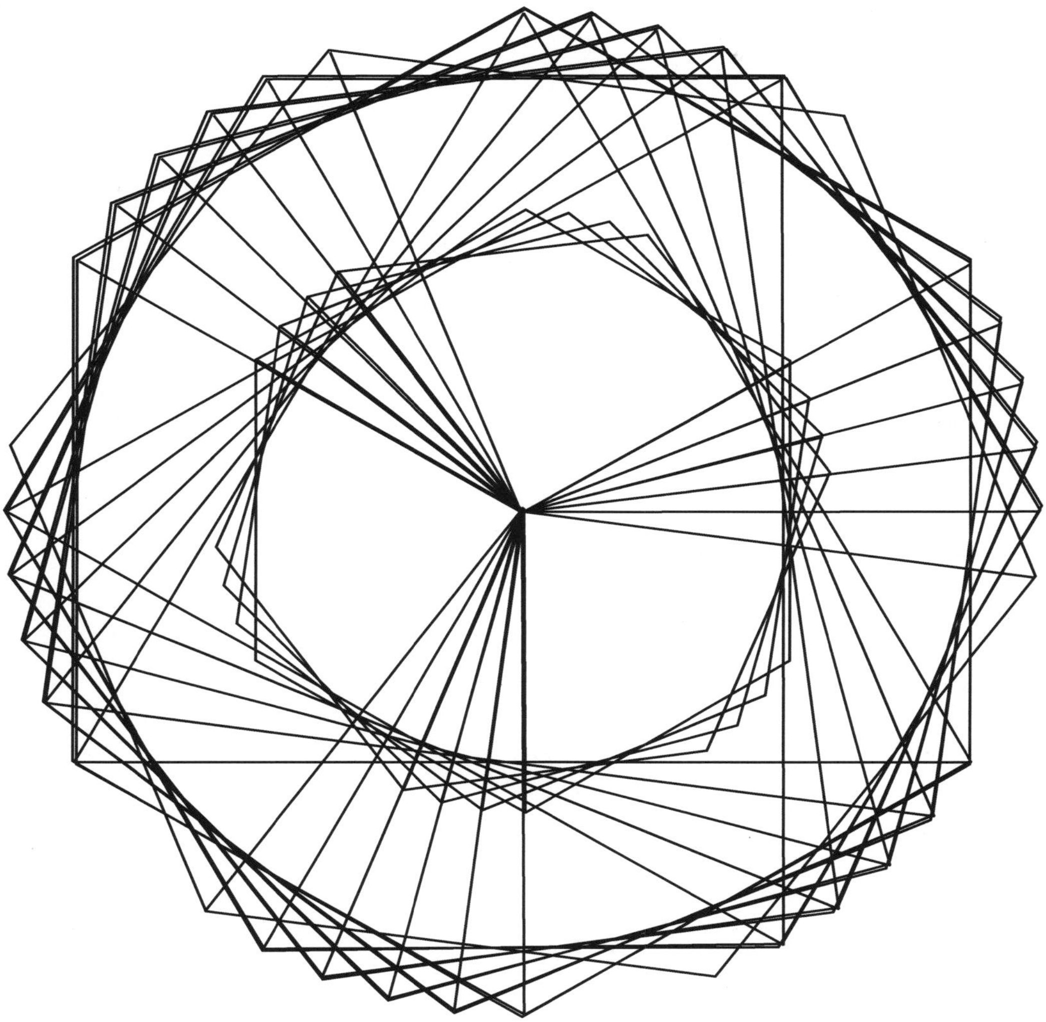

Female Balance

Mantra: SO FA TAY

Mandala Intention:

This code is used for balancing female energies and the female polarities of the body.

Assists in relieving PMS and cramps.

Beneficial for pregnant mothers, increases maternal instinct.

Recommendations:

Place in sick rooms.

Put on night lights or baby blankets. This will increase the feelings of security for the baby.

Good for mediation, massage, and therapeutic atmospheres.

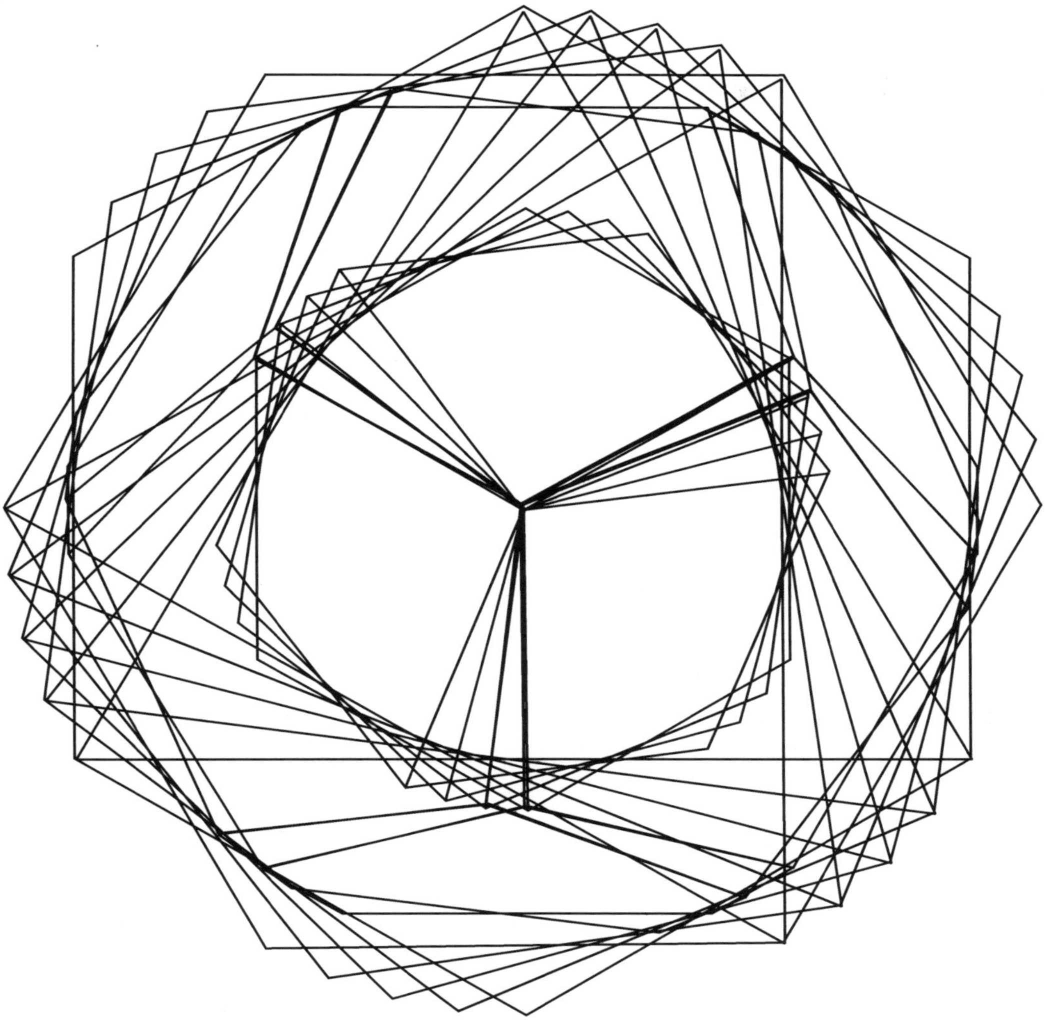

Male Balance

Mantra: SO TAY LA SO DOH

Mandala Intention:

The code is used to balance male energies and the male polarities of the body.

Beneficial energy physical activity, martial arts, teaching, working with women, doctors and new fathers.

Recommendations:

Place in baby rooms and gyms.

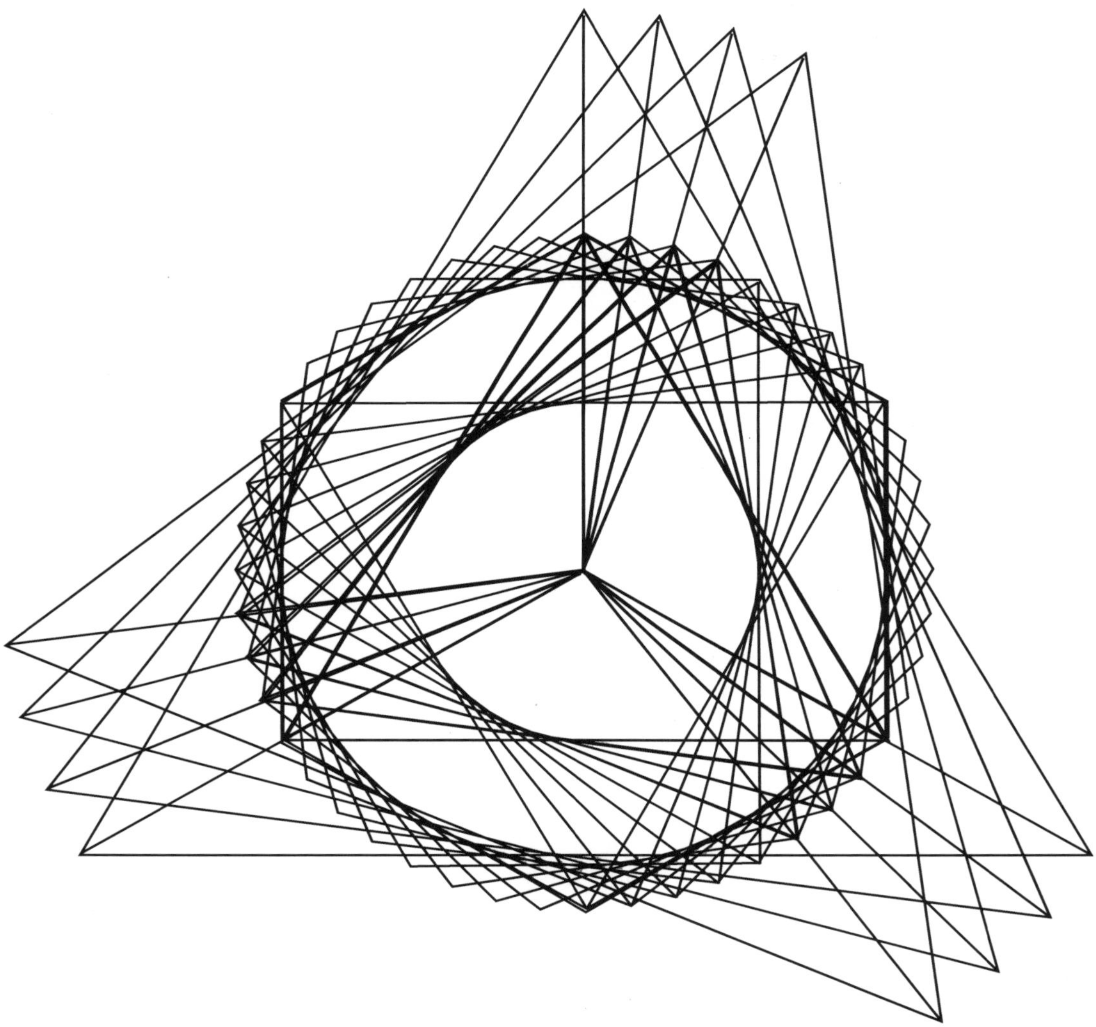

Protection

Mantra: SO LA TAY

Mandala Intention:

Protects and cloaks the aura with an energetic field to stop psychic attacks and any other non beneficial influences.

Recommendations:

This code can be placed in cars, planes and factories.

Sport athletes can wear this code to help prevent injuries.

Beneficial for traveling on planes and going to foreign countries.

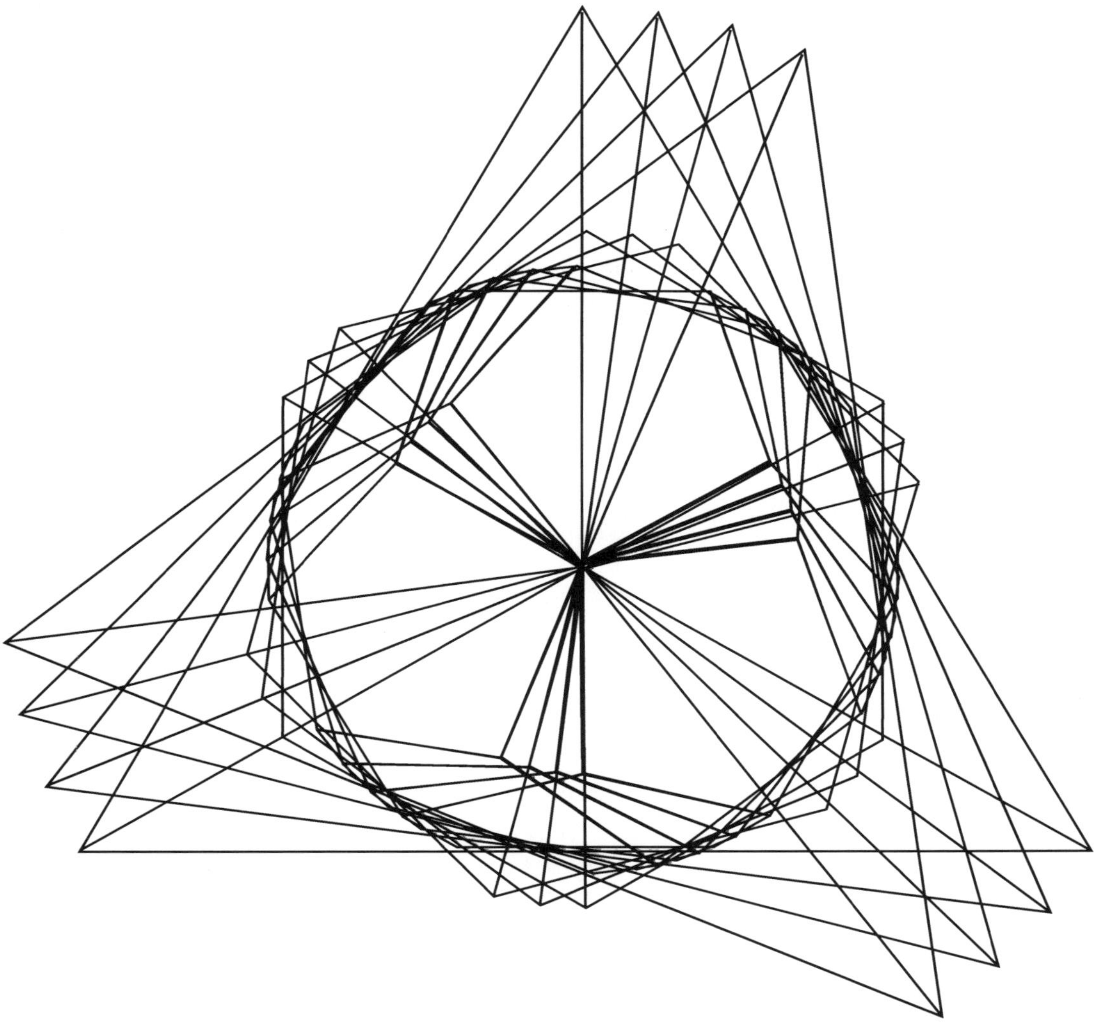

Psychic Protection

Mantra: SO LA

Mandala Intention:

This code protects all auric levels. The physical, Emotional, Mental and Etheric.

Beneficial for bad dreams, sleeping in hotels, meditation, astral projection travels and journeying.

Recommendations:

Place code on alter where you are meditating.

For sleeping, place on night stand or the headboard of bed.

Place under pillow for bad dreams.

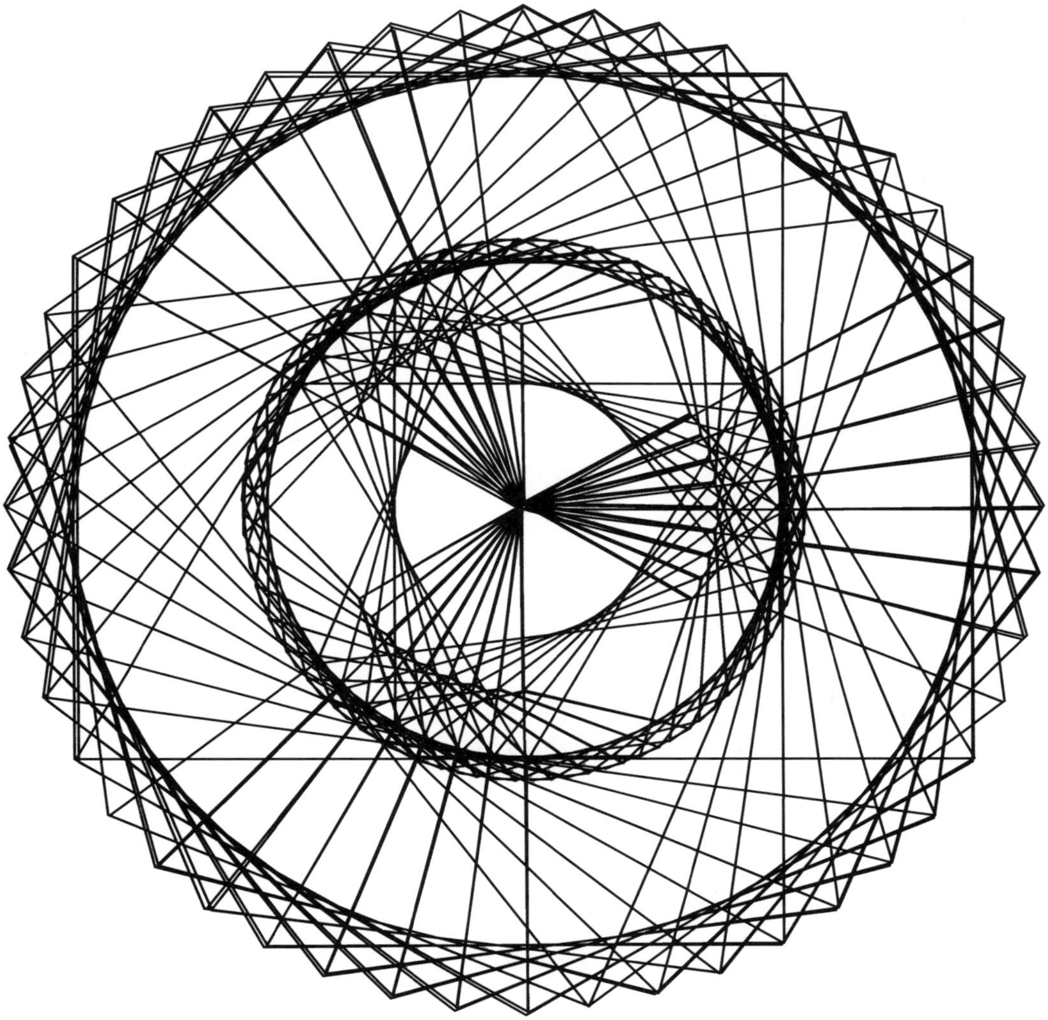

Code Of Ra

Mantra: SO LA SO

Mandala Intention:

This code connects us with the healing power of the sun. Ra can be used as a master healing code.

This energy is also beneficial for charging and changing the vibration of food.

Beneficial for people that suffer seasonal affective disorder.

Recommendations:

Place code on chakras while breathing in the energies of the sun.

Put under plate or glass to embed the healing energies of the sun into food and water.

Can meditate on before and after the "Salute to the Sun". (Egyptian Postures of Power - Qigong System)

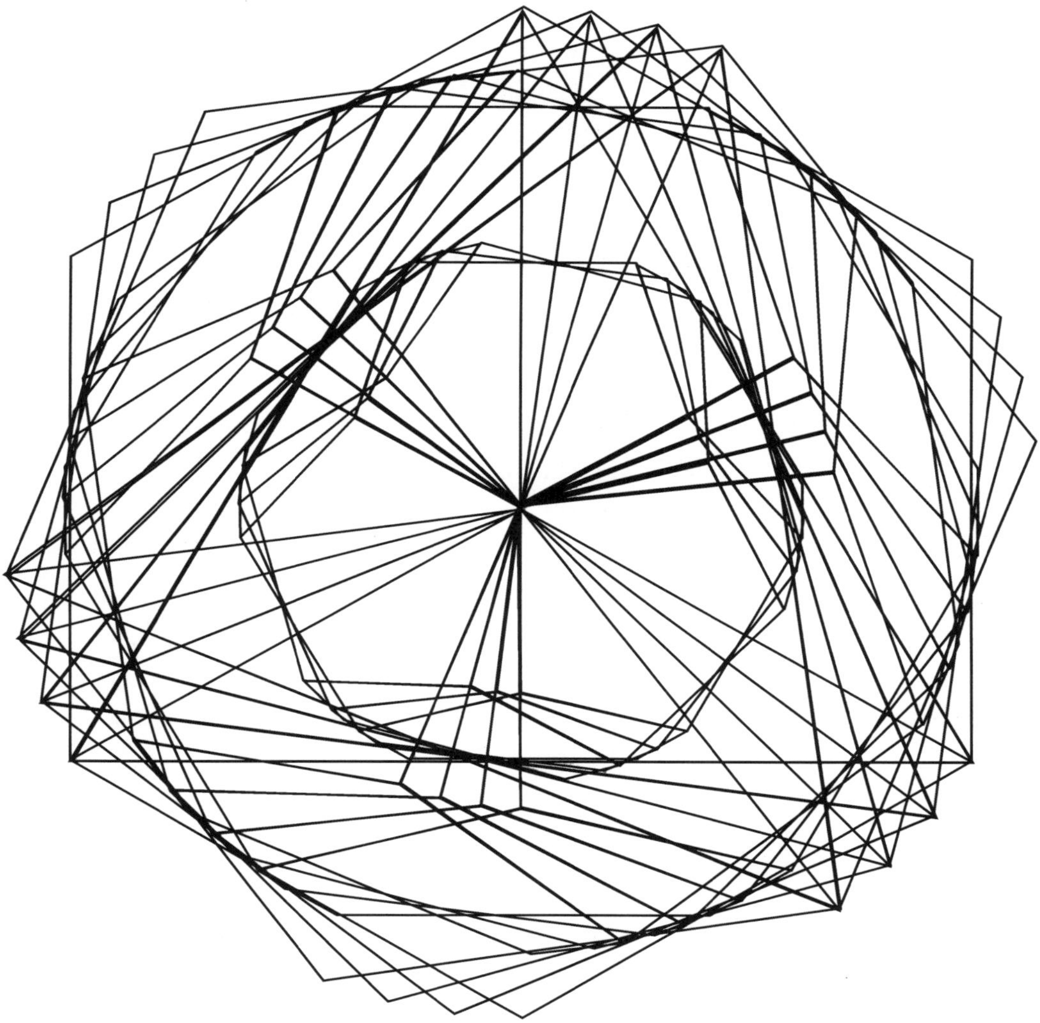

Code Of Amon

Mantra: SO TEE TEE

Mandala Intention:

This code is great for grounding energies into Mother Earth through our feet and chakra system.

Assists in mental activities, studying and retention. This code can be beneficial for students.

Recommendations:

Place code on third eye to bring clarity to the mind.

Meditating on this energy will bring greater focus and clarity to the mind.

Place on chakras to ground and heal lower vibrational energies.

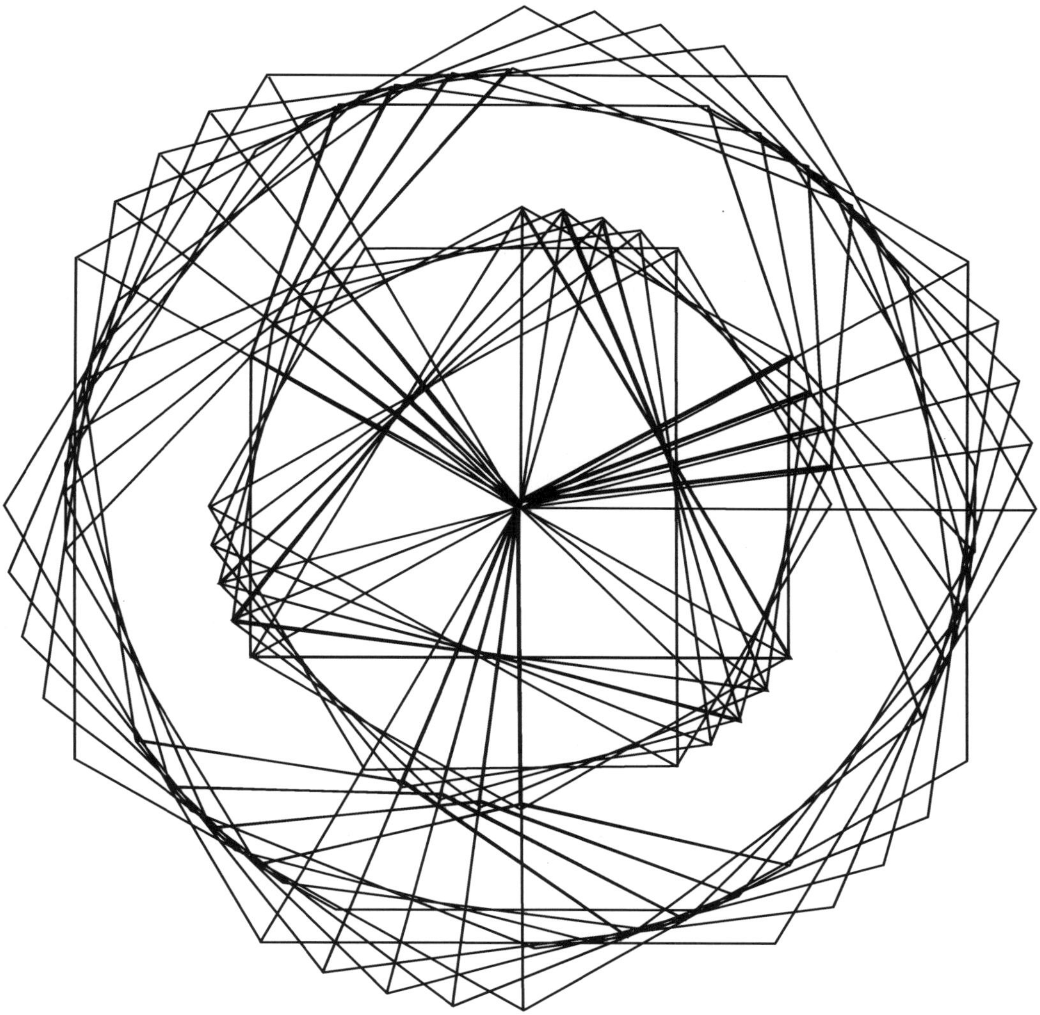

Angelic Realm

Mantra: LA LA SO

Mandala Intention:

This code can be used for protection and receiving messages from guardian angels while in meditation or journey states.

Can also be used to assists the energies of the lungs and breathing issues.

The energy of this code attracts fairies and earth divas into your space.

Recommendations:

Place code in cribs to help babies sleep and keep their energies protected.

Meditating on this energy will connect to the angelic realm to receive protection, messages, and guidance.

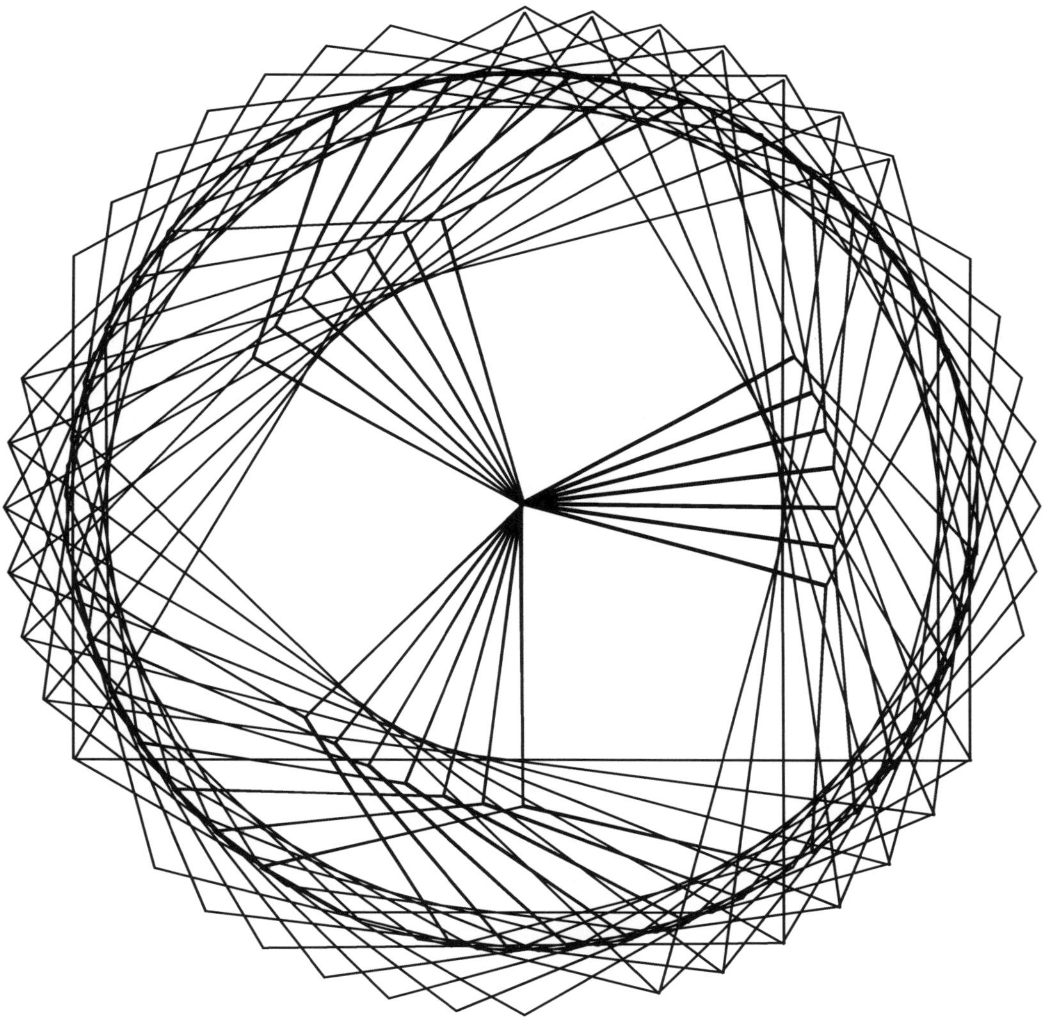

Higher Self

Mantra: LA LA TEE DOH

Mandala Intention:

This code can be used for clearing blockages.

Beneficial for group projects and team work. It unites groups of people so that they may work together.

Assists in reconciliations and conflicts.

Recommendations:

Place code in airplanes or public places so that people will feel less claustrophobic.

Meditating on this energy will assist the energetic bodies and chakras to release blocks and reconnect to the higher aspects of their true self.

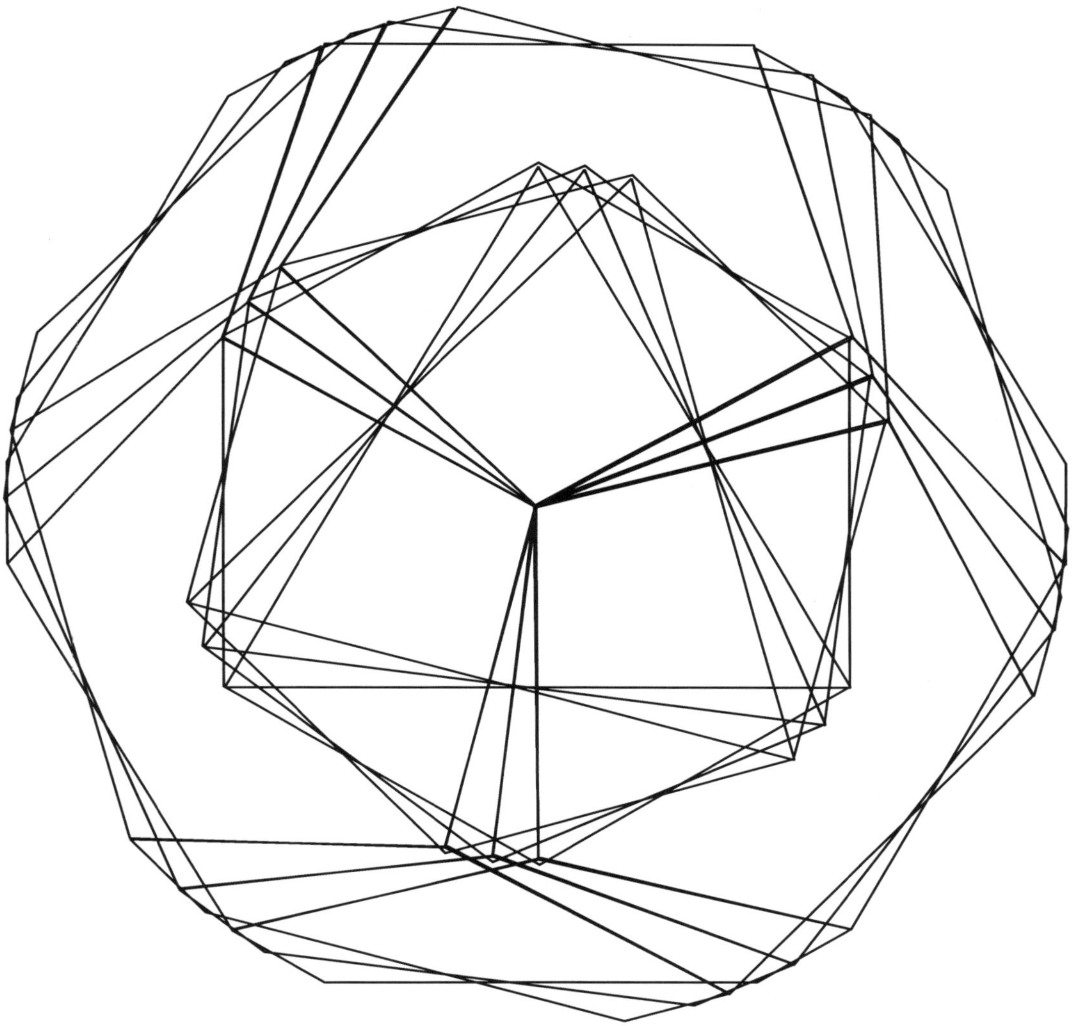

Harmony

Mantra: LA TEE SO LA

Mandala Intention:

This code can be used for orchestras, choirs, recording equipment and anything else music related to connect and integrate the higher frequencies of harmony within it.

Soothes a troubled spirit.

Recommendations:

Beneficial for running water and small fountains.

Assists in mixing oils and fragrances.

Can be placed on wind chimes.

The energy of this code would be beneficial to be placed in slaughter houses, cramped spaces, trains, cars and planes.

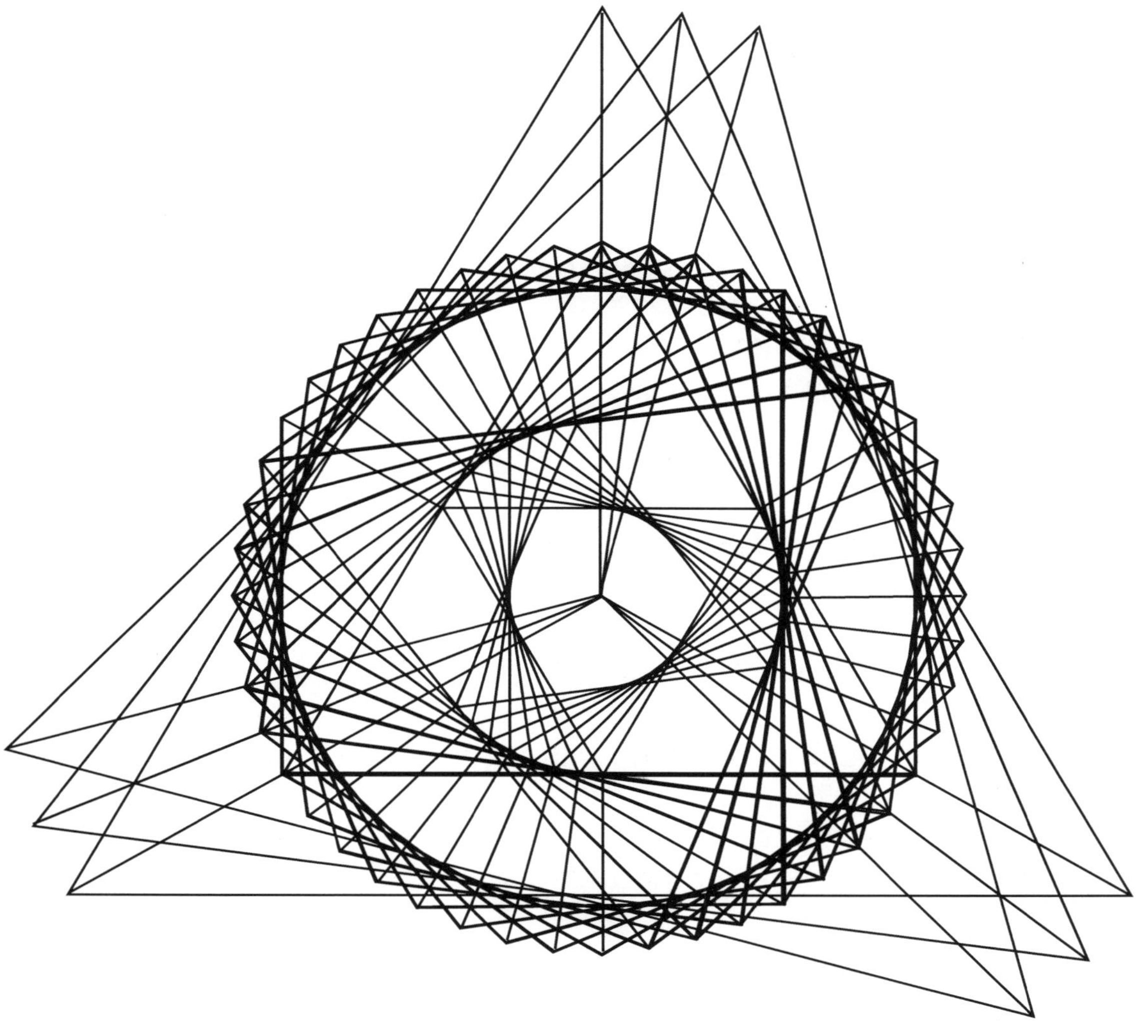

Compassion

Mantra: DOH DOH LA

Mandala Intention:

The code of compassion assists to harmonize our bodies chemistry of adrenaline and hormones.

The energies of this code enhances melatonin and serotonin from the endocrine system to relax our energetic system.

Beneficial in churches and spiritual groups.

Recommendations:

Wear after physical trauma or fights.

Beneficial for wrestlers, boxers and sports athletes.

Meditating on this energy will assist women in relieving PMS symptoms and cramps.

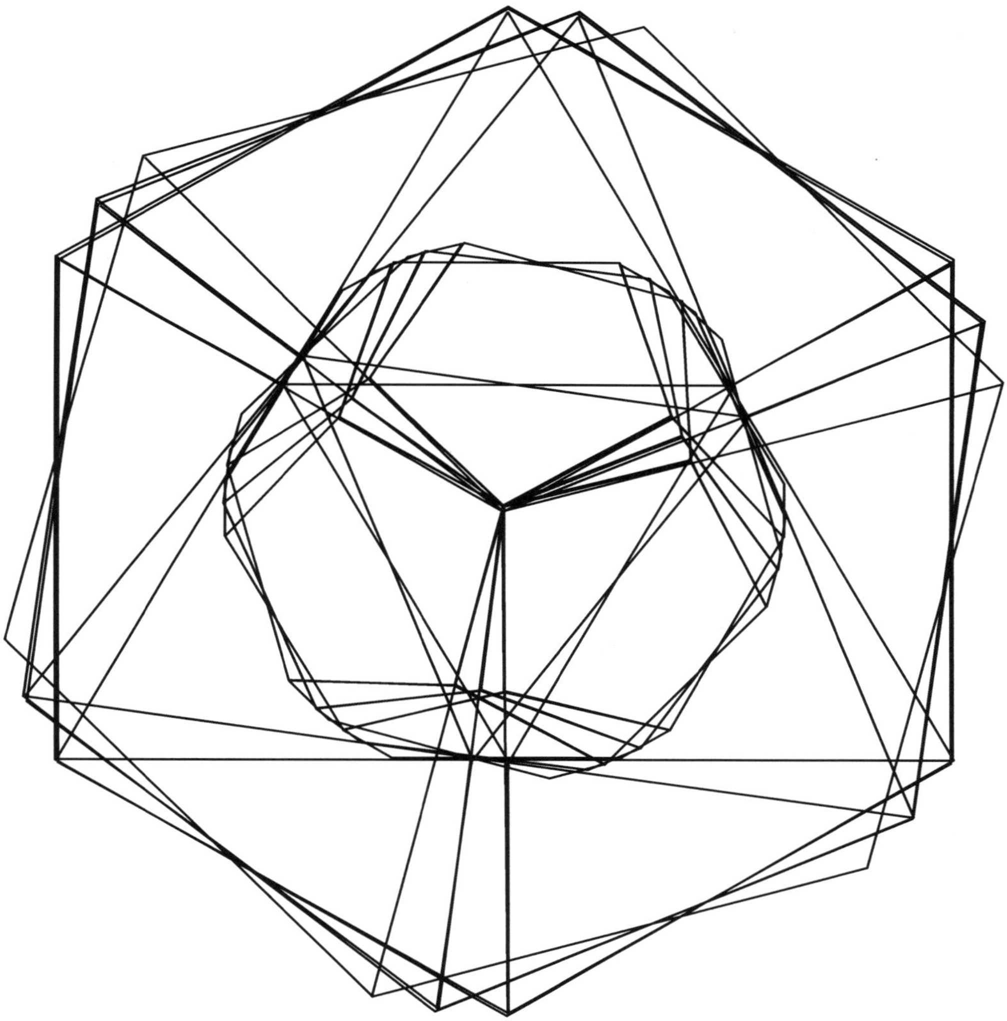

Forgiveness

Mantra: DOH TEE TEE LA

Mandala Intention:

This code helps to see the divine connection in all things.

The energy of this code is great for counseling.

Diffuses anger and assists in lowering blood pressure.

May be beneficial in relieving headaches.

Recommendations:

The energy of this code can be placed in churches, jails, polices stations, and hospitals.

Meditating on this code will assist the process of letting go of all the old wounds and thoughts that we carry with us.

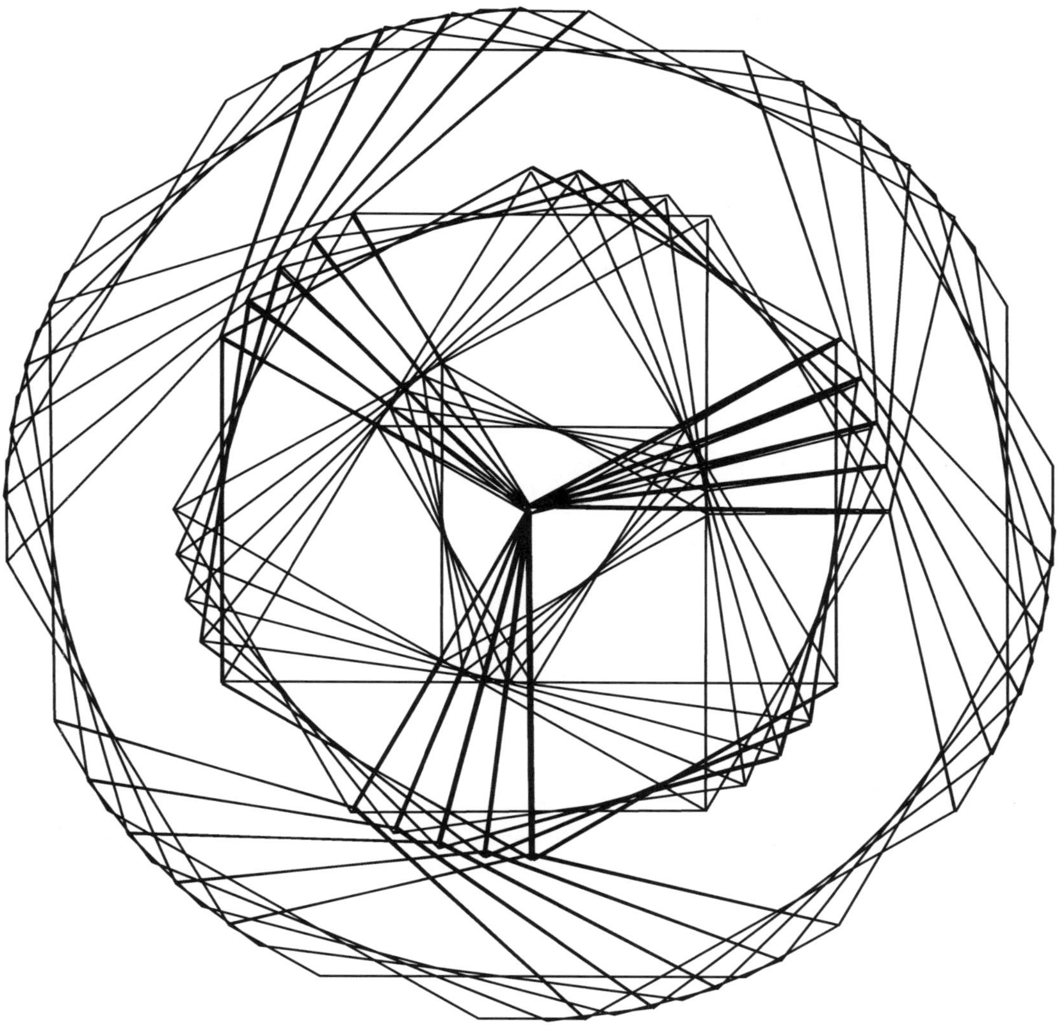

Centering

Mantra: DOH SO TEE LA

Mandala Intention:

The energy of this code enhances the work of artists and craftsmen, those working with earth materials.

Great for Feng Shui and interior design because this code enhances energy flow.

Recommendations:

Place on work sites or in work areas.

Place in the center of the room or in the corners to assist Feng Shui and energy flow.

Place on the heart and throat chakra before giving a speech to align your words and intentions.

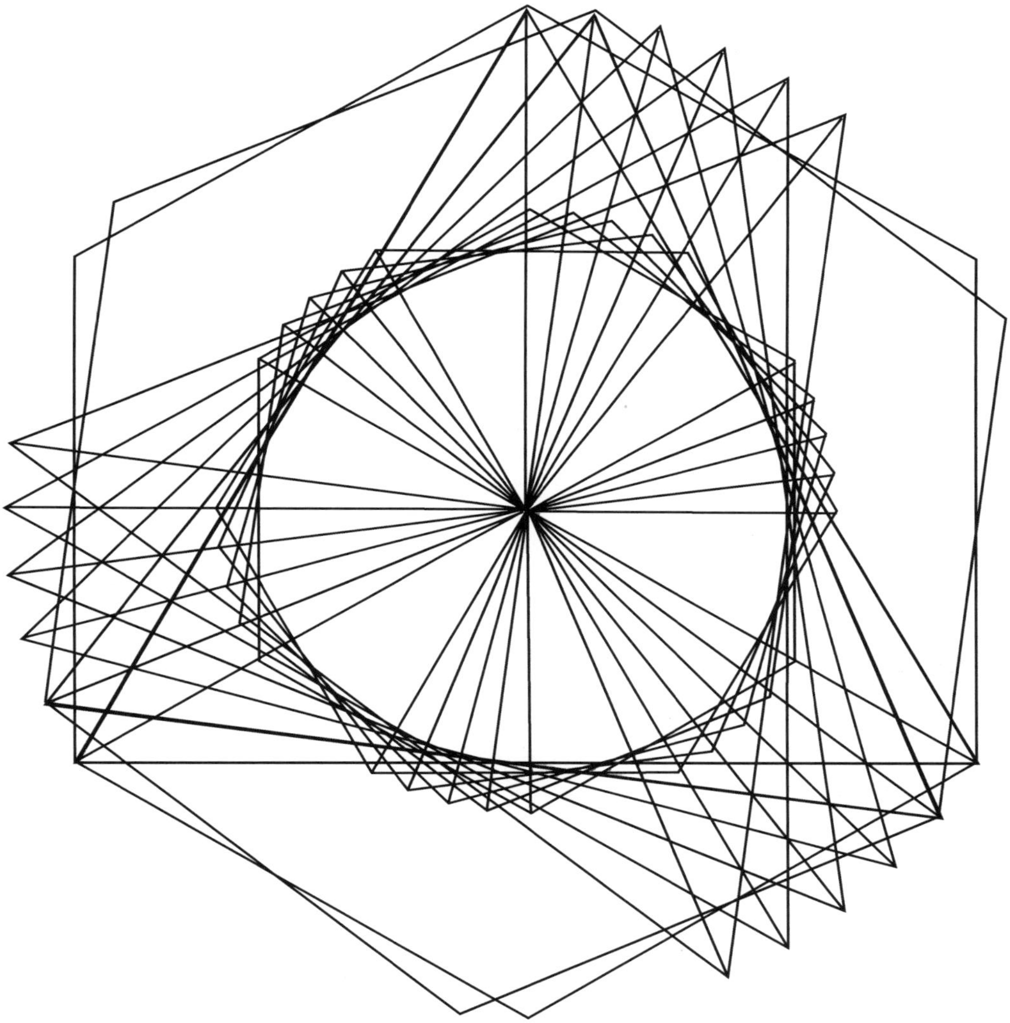

Water Transformer

Mantra: DOH ME LA

Mandala Intention:

This code is used energetically for the purification of water.

Changes structure of water to its highest vibrational level.

Helps remove energetic pollutants out of water.

Recommendations:

Visualize the water illuminating with red light, then blue light, then pink light. This will change the structure of the water.

Place under or on glass of water to encode these frequencies into it.

This code is good for aquarium tanks and anything else to do with water.

Can be placed next to or in moving water. (Rivers & streams)

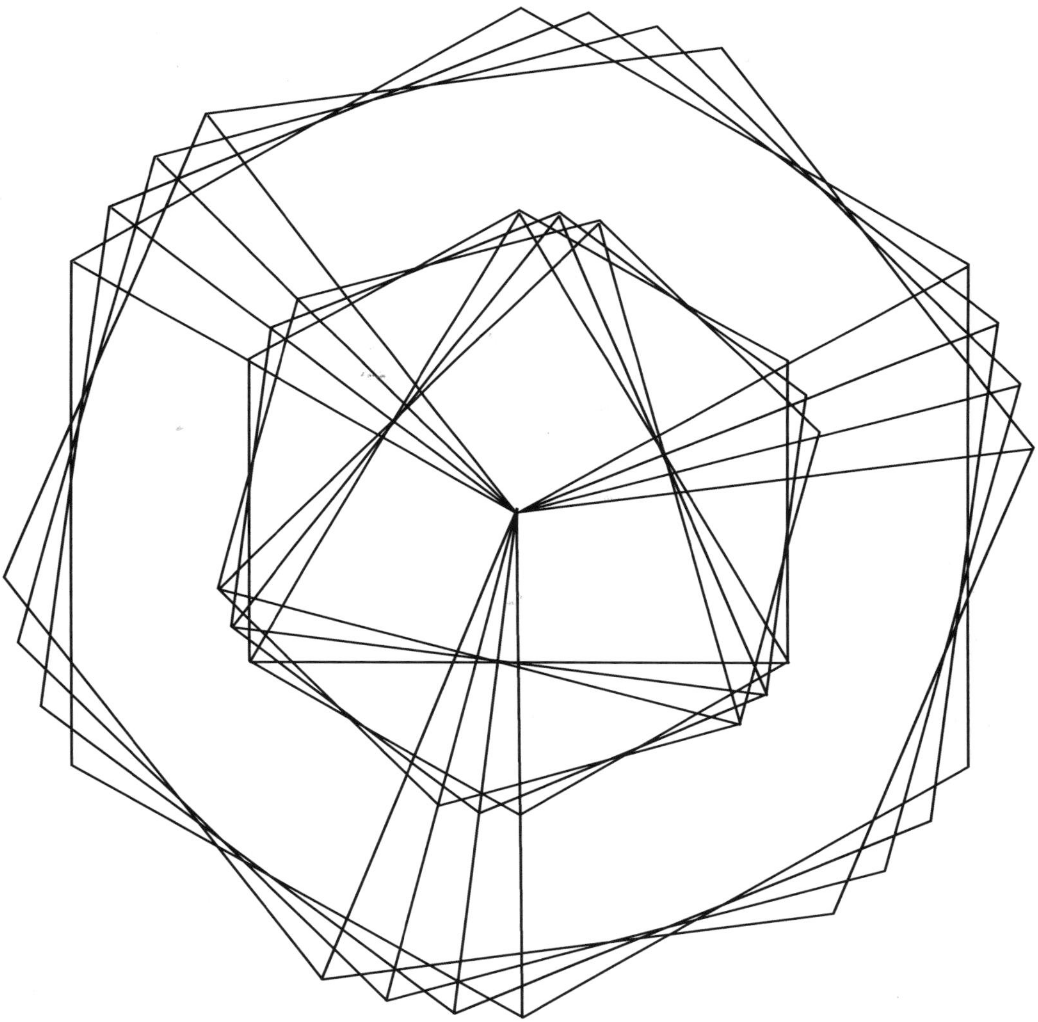

Food Transformer

Mantra: SO LA TA

Mandala Intention:

This code purifies and heals the atomic structure of food before consumption.

Beneficial for plants, helps remove toxins as they grow.

Recommendations:

Place hand over code for 20 seconds, then place hand over food for 20 seconds to transform the energies.

Code can be placed under plate, or any place where there is food, supplements or medicines.

You can program your food to fit your own personal needs.

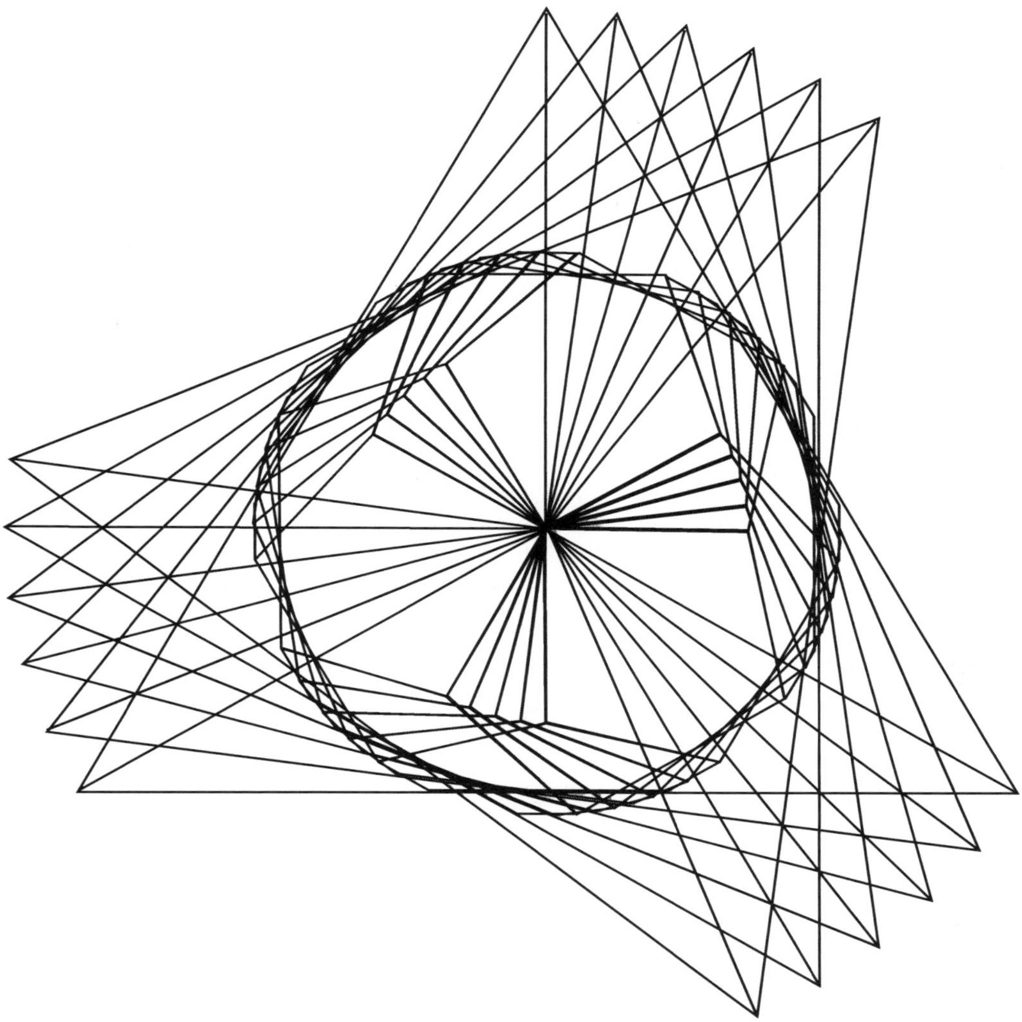

Earth Energy

Mantra: DOH ME SO TEE

Mandala Intention:

This code works on clearing lay lines and toxic earth energies.

Assist infertile soil to grow by bringing in fairies and earth divas.

This energy is also beneficial for extractions, house clearing, and exorcisms.

Recommendations:

Placing this code on the chakras will ground them into the earth and align them.

By placing this code into the earth, the energy will assist certain plants to grow in difficult soil conditions. (Setting your personal intention is also very important.)

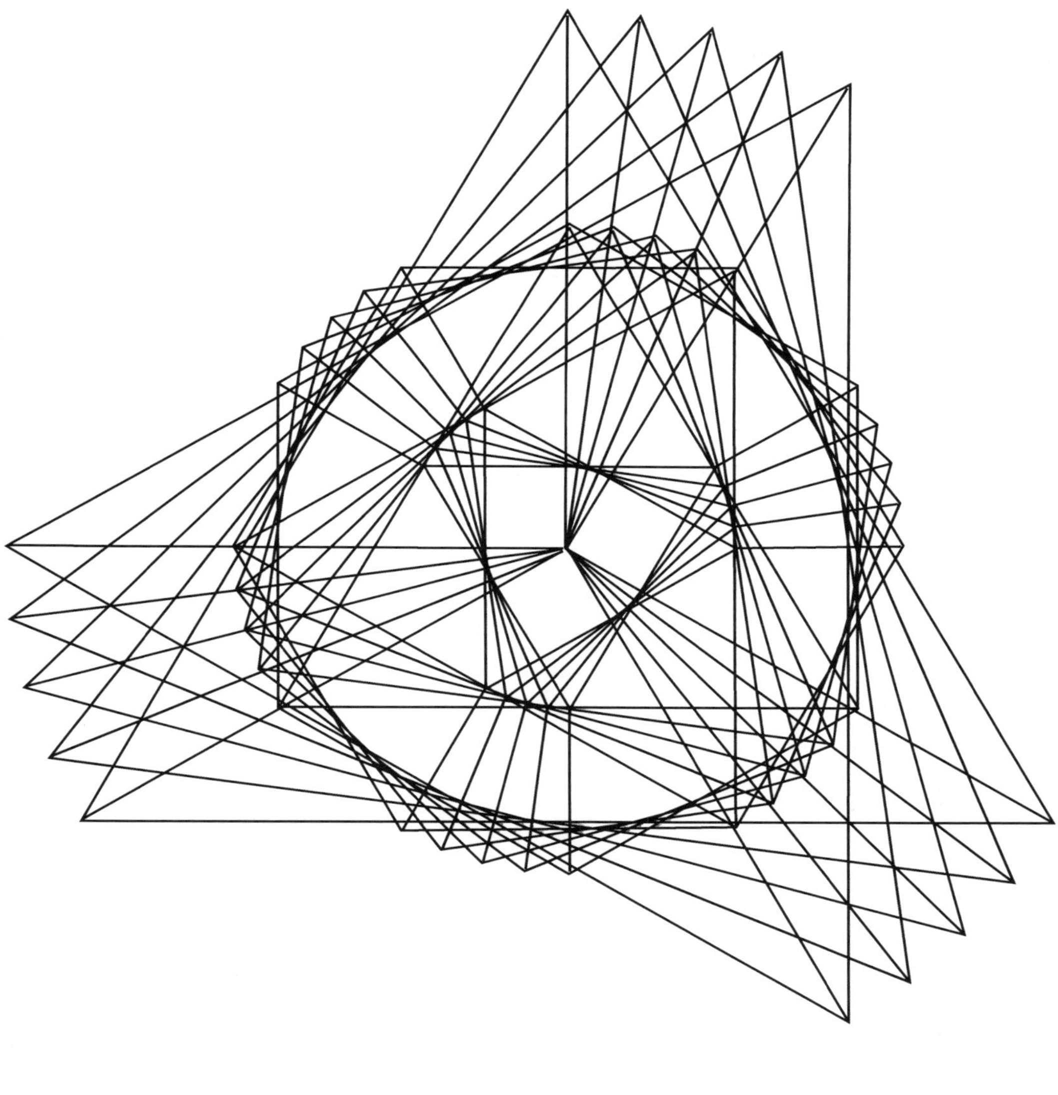

EMF Transformer

Mantra: TA LA

Mandala Intention:
This code assists in clearing the environment of electromagnetic radiation. The energy of this code creates a 100 foot field of protection in all directions.

Recommendations:
Place on four walls to clear closed environments.

Works well in computer rooms, cars, airplanes and factories.

Place on power boxes, cellphone towers and cell phones to shrink the harmful effects of EMF.

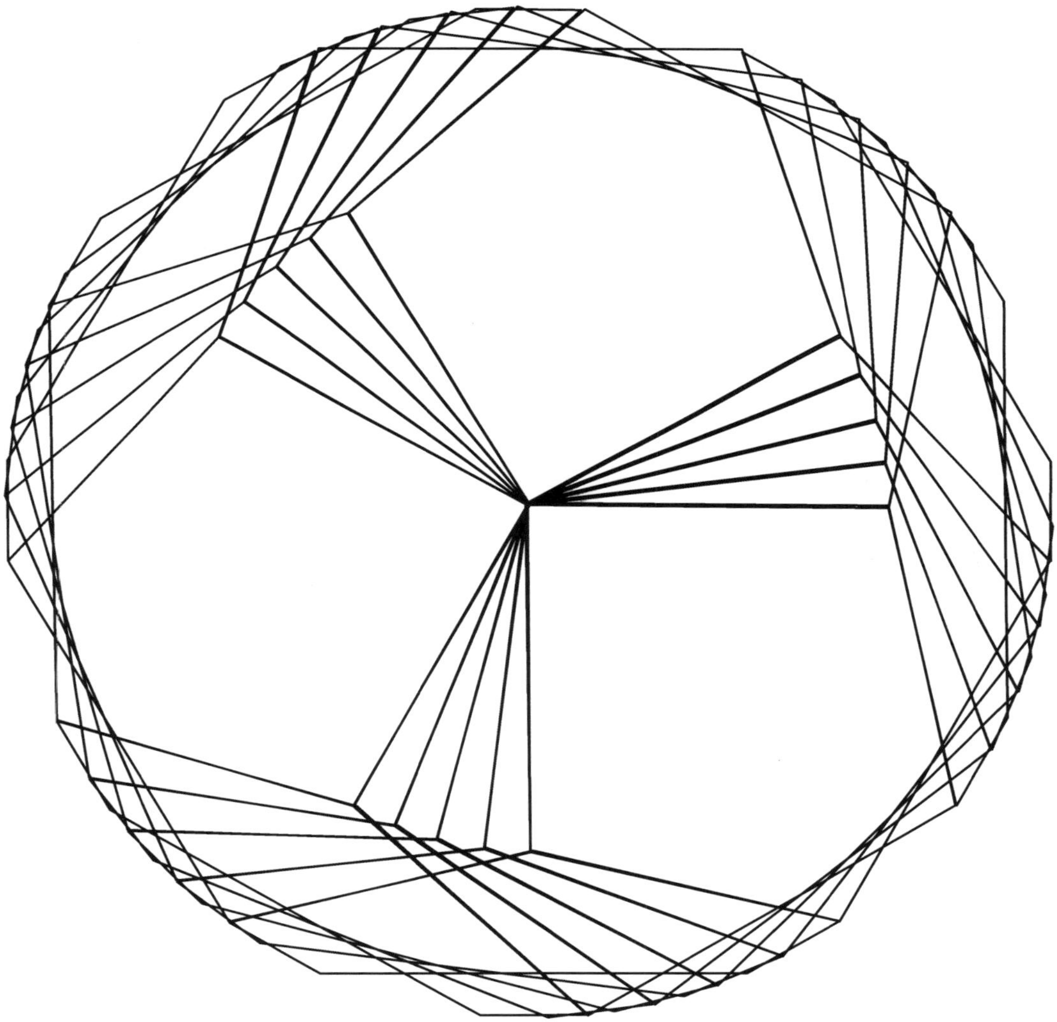

"If you only knew the magnificence of the 3, 6 and 9, then you would have a key to the universe."

– Nikola Tesla

The Flower Of Life Code: The Secret of 3,6,9

Lets have some fun with the numbers that make up the Flower Of life. First lets simply dissect the patterns that make up this symbol.

Here is a Flower Of Life grid. As you can see it is just made up of circles expanding exponentially from its center.

Lets break this down further and count the circles. We can now see that the Flower Of Life is expanding by the value of 6 in a hexagonal pattern. 6,12,18,24,30,36, etc.

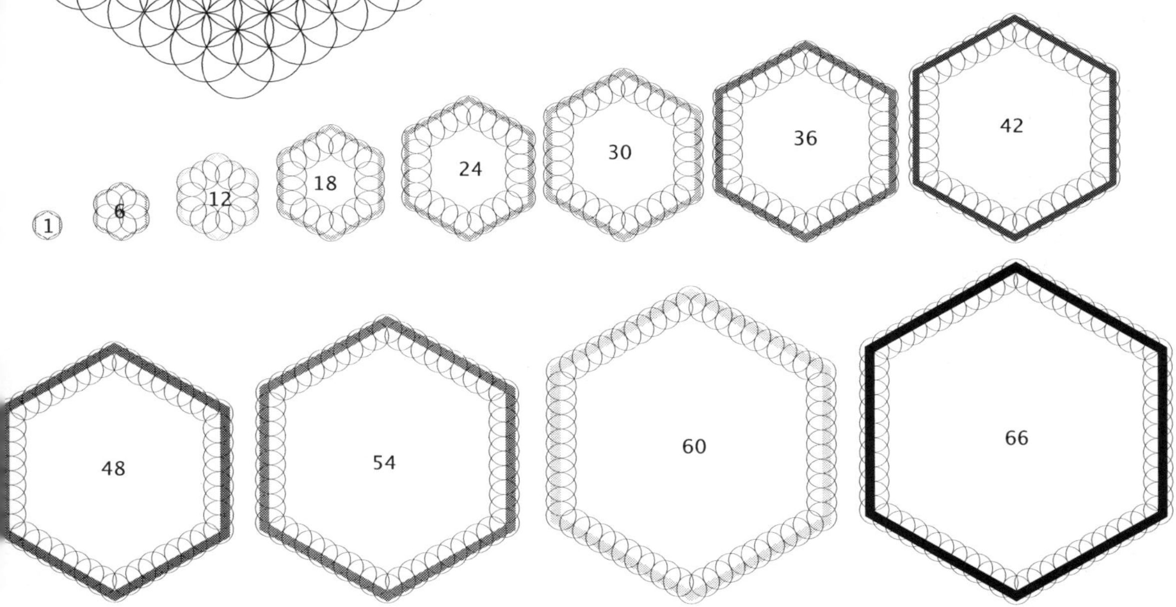

The Secret of 3,6,9

Now we have a straight forward sequence of numbers all based on the number 6. Lets lay this progression out and start to play with different combinations of these numbers using multiplication, division, addition and subtraction.

Wave Sequence 1

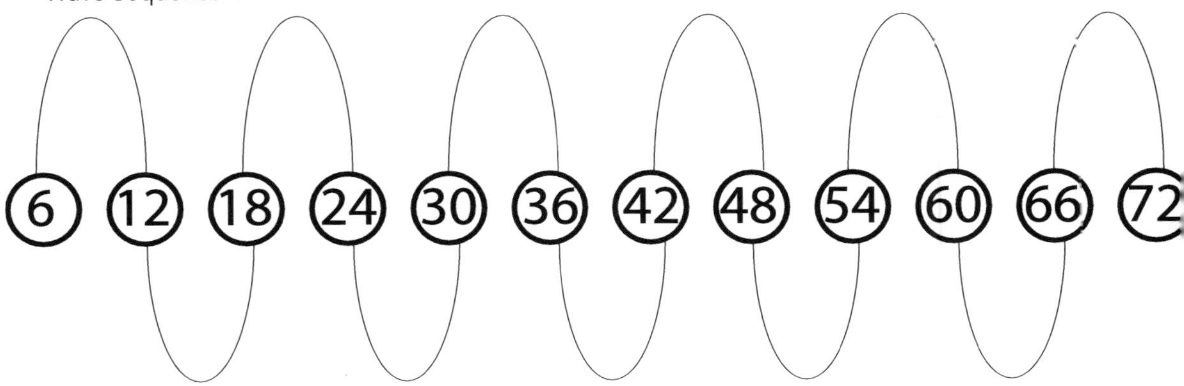

6x12 = **72** (7+2=**9**)

12x18 = **216** (2+1+6=**9**)

18x24 = **432** (4+3+2=**9**)

24x30 = **720** (7+2=**9**)

30x36 = **1,080** (1+8=**9**)

36x42 = **1,512** (1+5+1+2=**9**)

42x48 = **2,016** (2+1+6=**9**)

48x54 = **2,592** (2+5+9+2=18) (1+8=**9**)

54x60 = **3,240** (3+2+4=**9**)

60x66 = **3,960** (3+9+6=18) (1+8=**9**)

66x72 = **4,752** (4+7+5+2=18) (1+8=**9**)

6x12x18 = **1,296** (1+2+9+6 =18) (1+8=**9**)

12x18x24 = **5,184** (5+1+8+4=18) (1+8=**9**)

18x24x30 = **12,960** (1+2+9+6=18) (1+8=**9**)

24x30x36 = **25,920** (2+5+9+2=18) (1+8=**9**)

30x36x42 = **45,360** (4+5+3+6=18) (1+8=**9**)

36x42x48 = **72,576** (7+2+5+7+6=27) (2+7=**9**)

42x48x54 = **108,864** (1+8+8+6+4=27) (2+7=**9**)

48x54x60 = **155,520** (1+5+5+5+2=18) (1+8=**9**)

54x60x66 = **213,840** (2+1+3+8+4=18) (1+8=**9**)

60x66x72 = **285,120** (2+8+5+1+2=18) (1+8=**9**)

If you take any one of the numbers of the sequence 6, 12, 18, 24, 30, 36, 42, 48, 54, 60, 66, 72 and divide it by 3. You will notice that another pattern emerges. 3 will only divide one time cleanly up until the 12th number (72) then the sequence continues this repeating pattern.

Wave Sequence 2

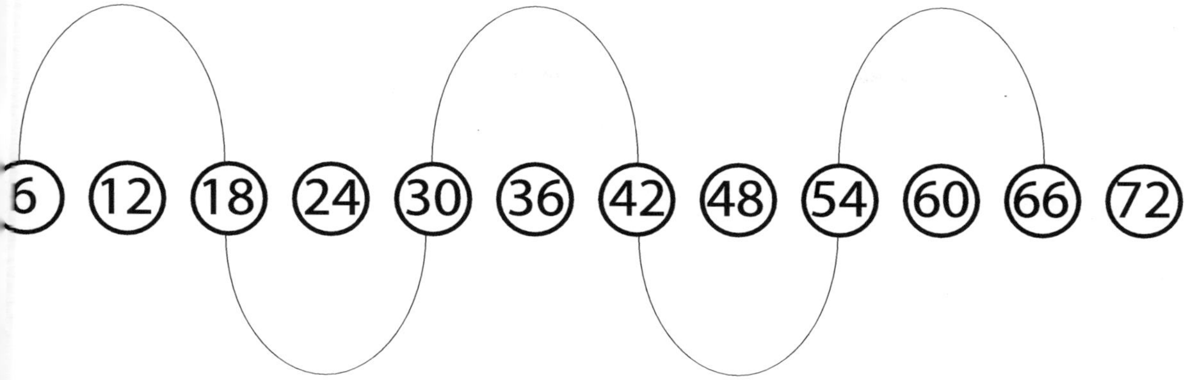

6x18 = **108** (1+8=**9**)
18x30 = **540** (5+4=**9**)
30x42 = **432** (4+3+2=**9**)
42x54 = **1,260** (1+2+6=**9**)
54x66 = **3,564** (3+5+6+4=**18**) (1+8=**9**)

6x18x30 = **3,240** (3+4+2 =**9**)
18x30x42 = **22,680** (2+2+6+8=18) (1+8=**9**)
30x42x54 = **68,040** (6+8+4=18) (1+8=**9**)
42x54x66 = **149,688** (1+4+9+6+8+8=36)(3+6=**9**)

Wave Sequence 3

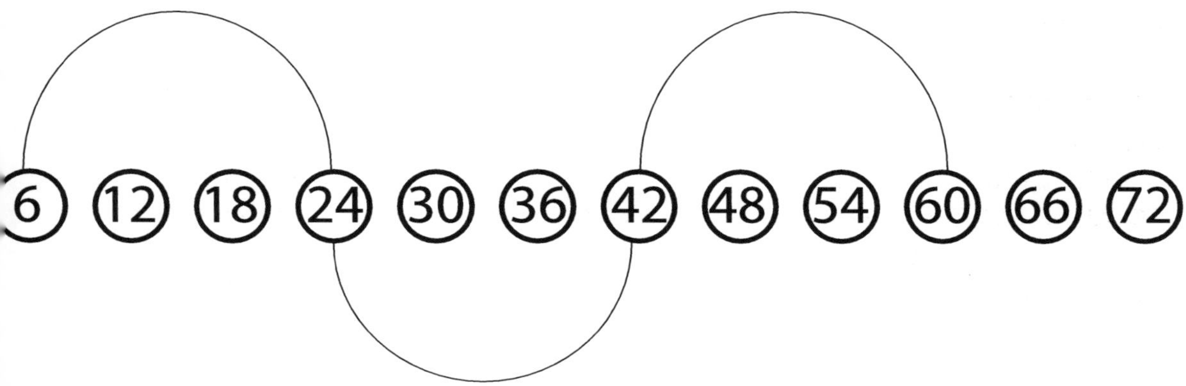

6x24 = **144** (1+4+4=**9**)
24x42 = **1,008** (1+8=**9**)
42x60 = **2,520** (2+5+2=**9**)

6x24x42 = **6,048** (6+4+8=**18**) (1+8=**9**)
24x42x60 = **22,680** (2+2+6+8=**18**) (1+8=**9**)

The beautiful thing about this code is you can pick any sequence you can think of and it will reveal spiritually significant numbers. For example lets chart a wave (24, 60) and (6,12,18, 24). Lets see what numbers they reveal.

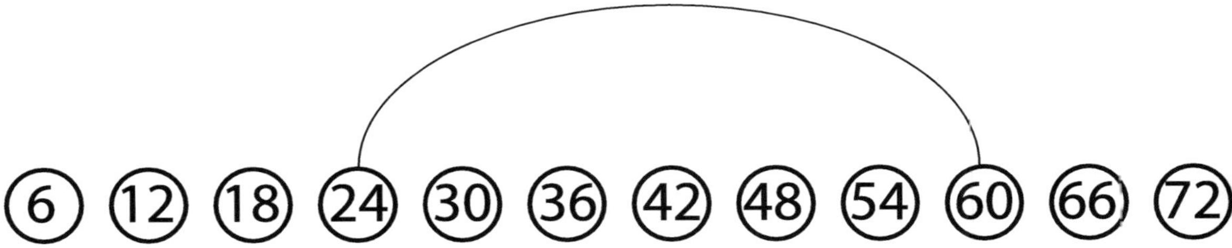

We can also lay out this formula using the structure of the Flower Of life.

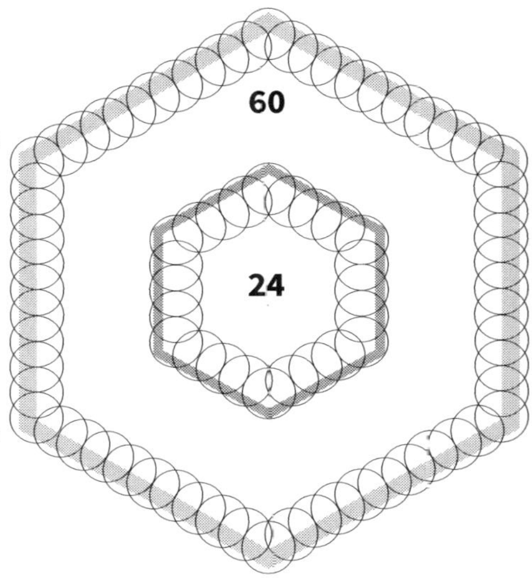

24x60 = **1,440** (Minutes in one day)
1440x60 = **86,400** (Seconds in a day)
1440/60 = **24** (Hours per day)

We can then say that this image represents the cycle of time in one earth day.

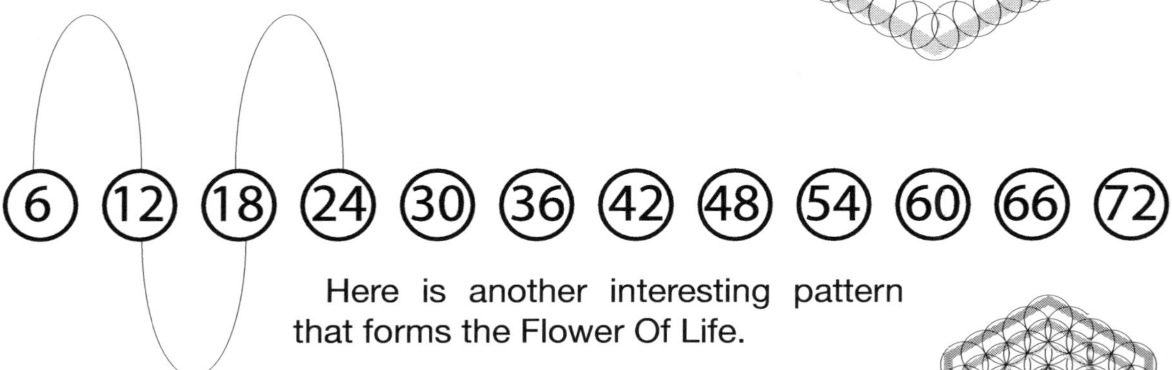

Here is another interesting pattern that forms the Flower Of Life.

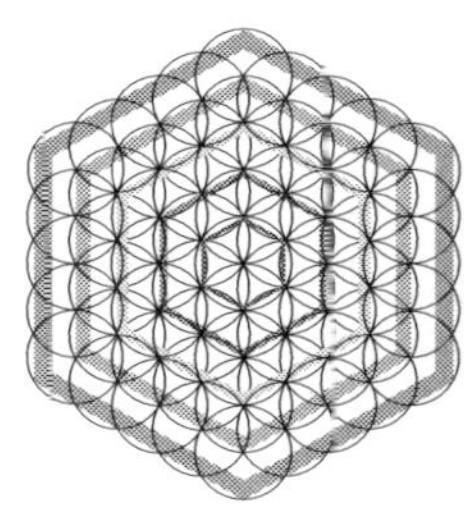

6x12x18x24 = **31,104**

In Hindu tradition they say that one year in the life of Brahma is 31,104 years.

As we can see, the numbers that are produced from the Flower Of Life Code are significant and hold secret knowledge. We can find these numbers hidden in sacred traditions from all over the world. From Egypt to the Aztecs, these numbers have been hidden in Kabbalah, Bible, Mayan calendar, Temple architecture, astrology and of course the nature of the universe.

Nikola Tesla was correct in saying *"If you only knew the magnificence of the 3, 6 and 9, then you would have a key to the universe."* It is through the Flower Of Life code that we can map out the numbers of heaven, Earth and all thats in between.

Here are a couple more examples.

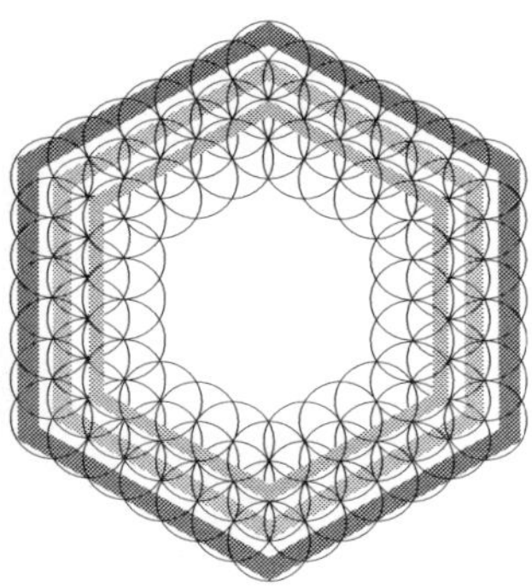

24x30x36 = 25,920

Planetary Cycle Code:
24x30x36 = **25,920** (Harmonic of planetary time)
It takes 25,920 years to complete the 12 cycle of the zodiac.

25,920/24 = **1080** (Moons radius in miles)
25,920/30 = **864** (Harmonic of the sun and heart)
25,920/36 = **720** (The sum of all angles of a Tetrahedron)

12/25,920 = **2,160** years per age
(The moon's diameter is also **2,160** miles.)

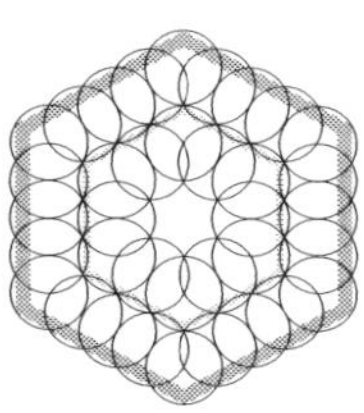

18x24 = 432

Light Code:
18x24 = **432** (the harmonic of light)
432 squared = **186,624** (the speed of light)
432x2 = **864** (the harmonic of the sun)

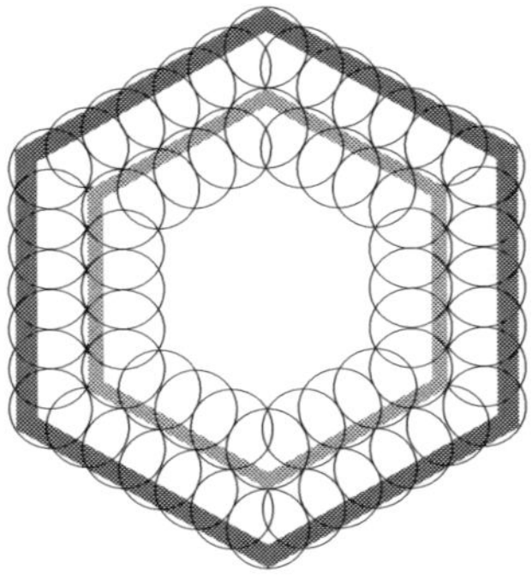

24x36 = 864

Sun Code:

24x36 = **864**
The Sun's diameter is **864,000** miles.
The average persons heart also beats **8,640** times a day.

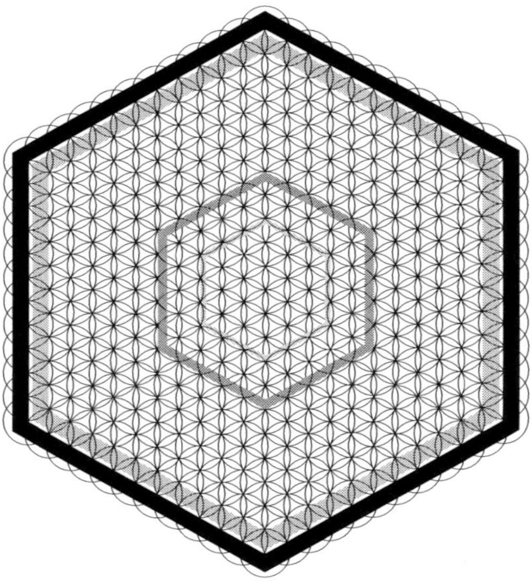

12x24 = 216
12x66 = 792
60x66 = 3960

Earth Code:

12x24 = **216** (Harmonic of the Earth)
(The numbers 666 can also be viewed as the Eart
(6x6x6 = **216**)
The circumference of the earth is **21,600** miles.

60x66 = **3960** (Radius of the Earth)

12x66 = **792** (Earths diameter is 7920 miles)

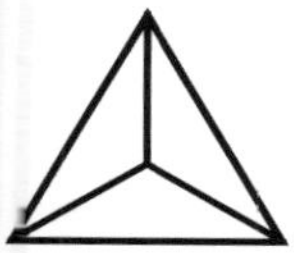

Tetrahedron
Faces: 4
Angle: 60
Sum Of Face Angles: 180
Sum Of Angles: 720

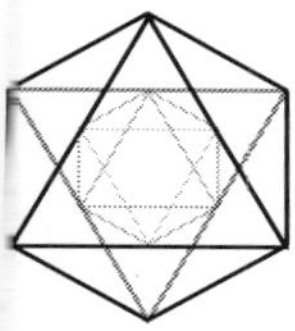

Octahedron
Faces: 8
Angle: 60
Sum Of Face Angles: 180
Sum Of Angles: 1440

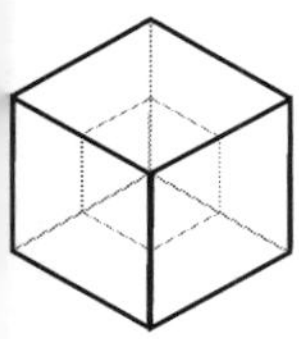

Cube
Faces: 6
Angle: 60
Sum Of Face Angles: 360
Sum Of Angles: 2160

Dodecahedron
Faces: 12
Angle: 60
Sum Of Face Angles: 540
Sum Of Angles: 6480

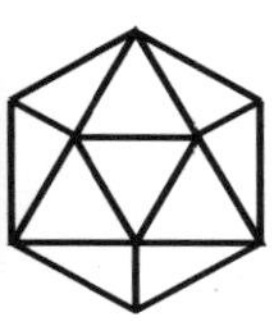

Icosahedron
Faces: 20
Angle: 60
Sum Of Face Angles: 180
Sum Of Angles: 3600

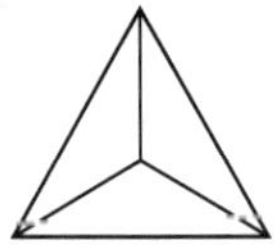 tetrahedron (fire – 4 faces)	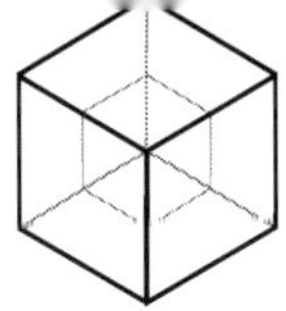 cube (earth – 6 faces)	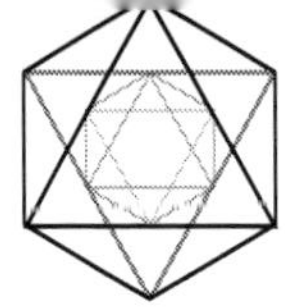 octahedron (air – 8 faces)	 dodecahedron (ether – 12 sided)	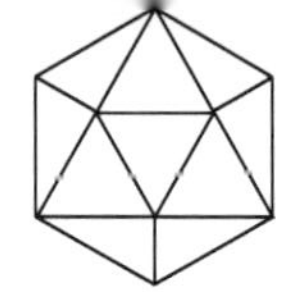 icosahedron (water – 20 sided)
6x4 =24	6x6 =36	6x8 =48	6x12 =72	6x20 =120
6x12x4 =288	6x12x6 =432	6x12x8 =576	6x12x12 =864	6x12x20 =1440
6x18x4 = 432	6x18x6 = 648	6x18x8 = 864	6x18x12 = 1296	6x18x20 = 2160
6x24x4 = 576	6x24x6 = 864	6x24x8 = 1152	6x24x12 = 3456	6x24x20 = 2880
6x30x4 = 720	6x30x6 = 1080	6x30x8 = 1440	6x30x12 = 2160	6x30x20 = 3600
6x36x4 = 864	6x36x6 = 1296	6x36x8 = 1728	6x36x12 = 2592	6x36x20 = 4320
12x4 = 48	12x6 = 72	12x8 = 96	12x12 = 144	12x20 = 240
12x18x4 = 864	12x18x6 = 1290	12x18x8 = 1728	12x18x12 = 2592	12x18x20 = 4320
12x24x4 = 1152	12x24x6 = 1728	12x24x8 = 2304	12x24x12 = 3456	12x24x20 = 5760
12x30x4 = 1440	12x30x6 = 2160	12x30x8 = 2880	12x30x12 = 4320	12x30x20 = 7200
12x36x4 = 1728	12x36x6 = 2592	12x36x8 = 2592	12x36x12 = 5184	12x36x20 = 8640
18x4 = 72	18x6 = 108	18x8 = 108	18x12 = 216	18x20 = 360
18x24x4 = 1728	18x24x6 = 2592	18x24x8 = 2592	18x24x12 = 5184	18x24x20 = 8640
18x30x4 = 2160	18x30x6 = 3240	18x30x8 = 3240	18x30x12 = 6480	18x30x20 = 10800
18x36x4 = 2592	18x36x6 = 3888	18x36x8 = 3456	18x36x12 = 7776	18x36x20 = 12960
24x4 = 96	24x6 = 144	24x8 =192	24x12 =288	24x20 =480
24x30x4 = 2880	24x30x6 = 4320	24x30x8 = 5760	24x30x12 = 8640	24x30x20 = 14400
24x36x4 = 3456	24x36x6 = 5184	24x36x8 = 6912	24x36x12 = 10368	24x36x20 = 17280
6x18x30x4 = 12960	6x18x30x6 = 19440	6x18x30x8 = 25920	6x18x30x12 = 38880	6x18x30x20 = 64800
12x24x36x4 = 41472	12x24x36x6 = 62208	12x24x36x8 = 82944	12x24x36x12 = 124416	12x24x36x20 = 207360

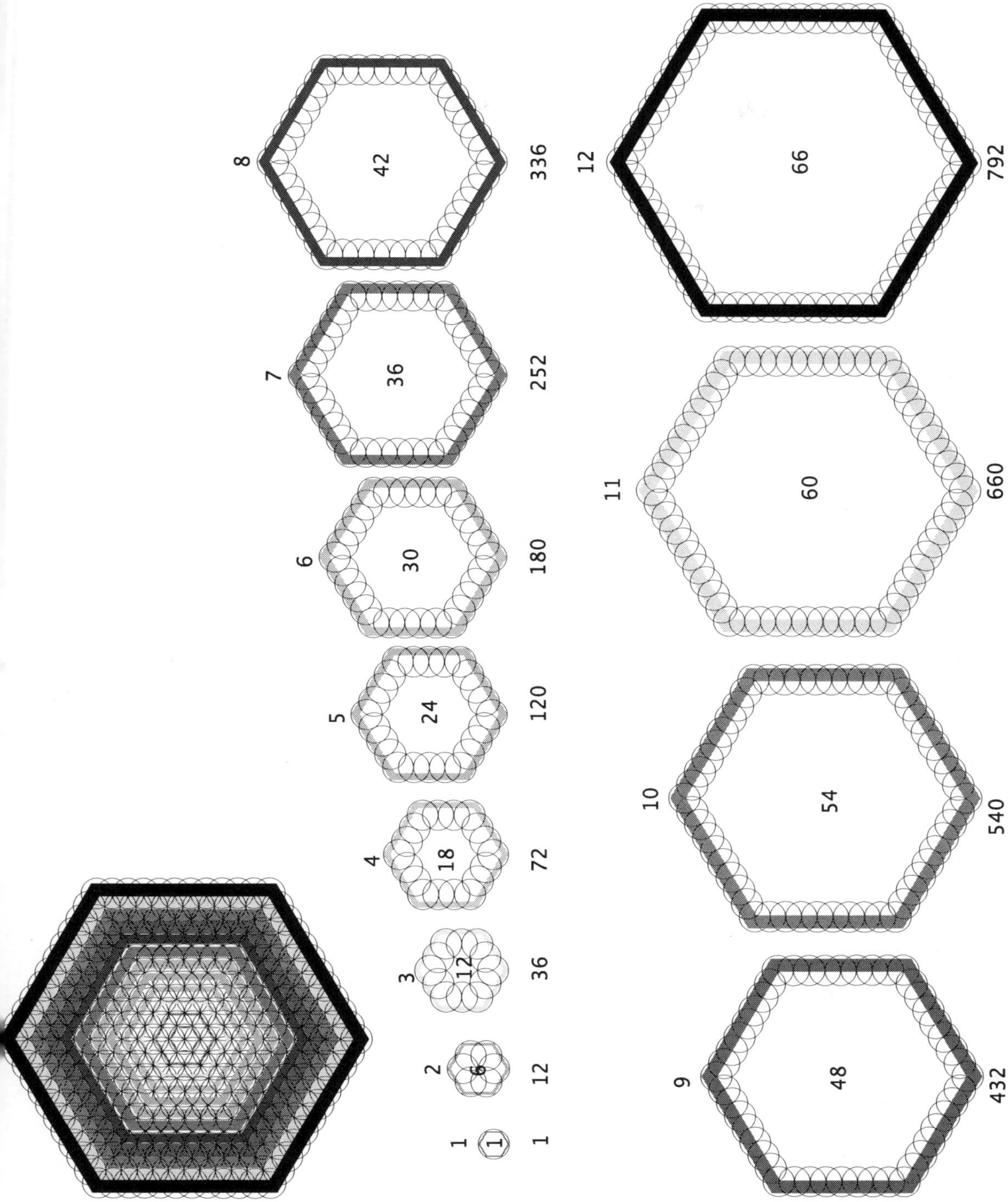
1 1 1
2 6 12
3 12 36
4 18 72
5 24 120
6 30 180
7 36 252
8 42 336
9 48 432
10 54 540
11 60 660
12 66 792

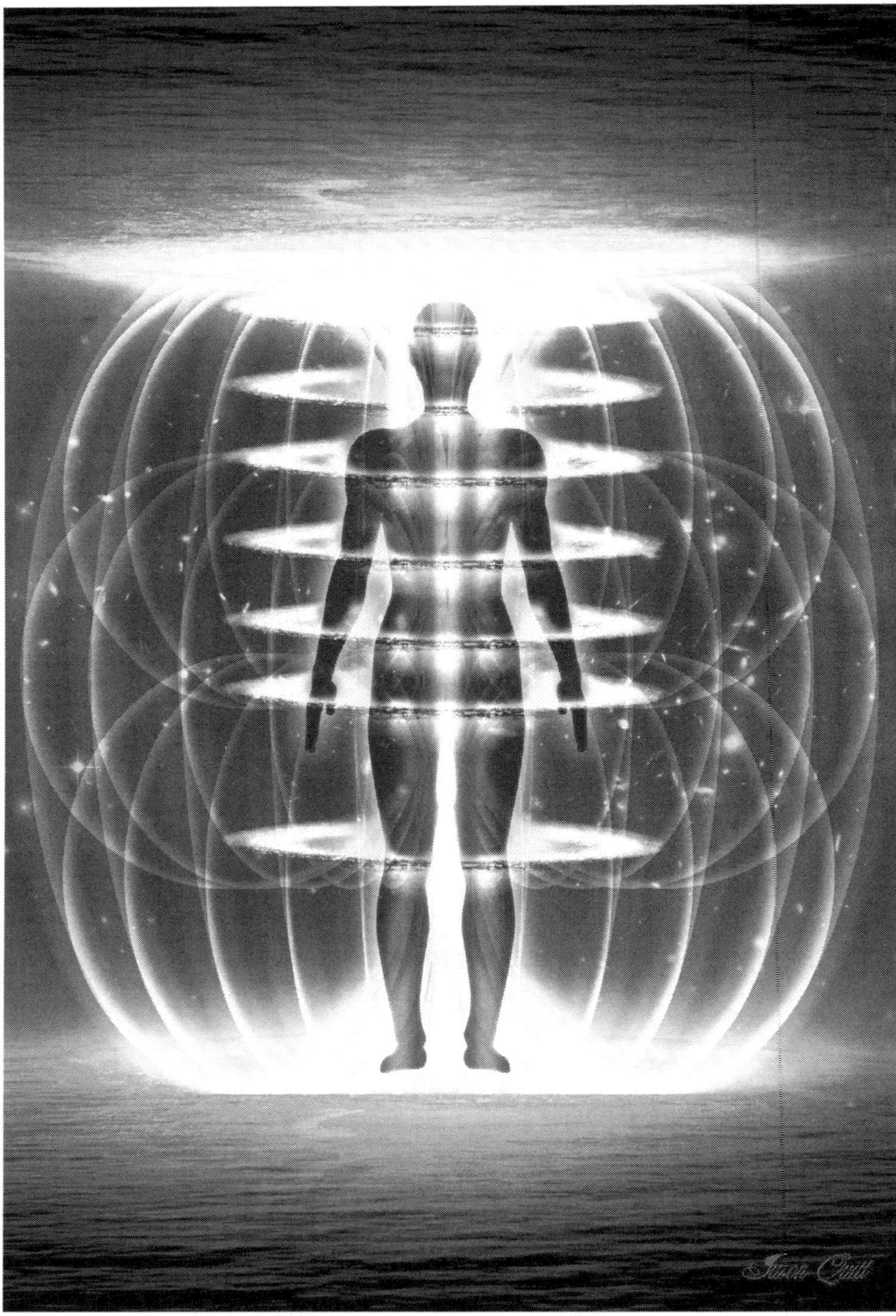
Jason Quitt's original artwork of the energy bodies.

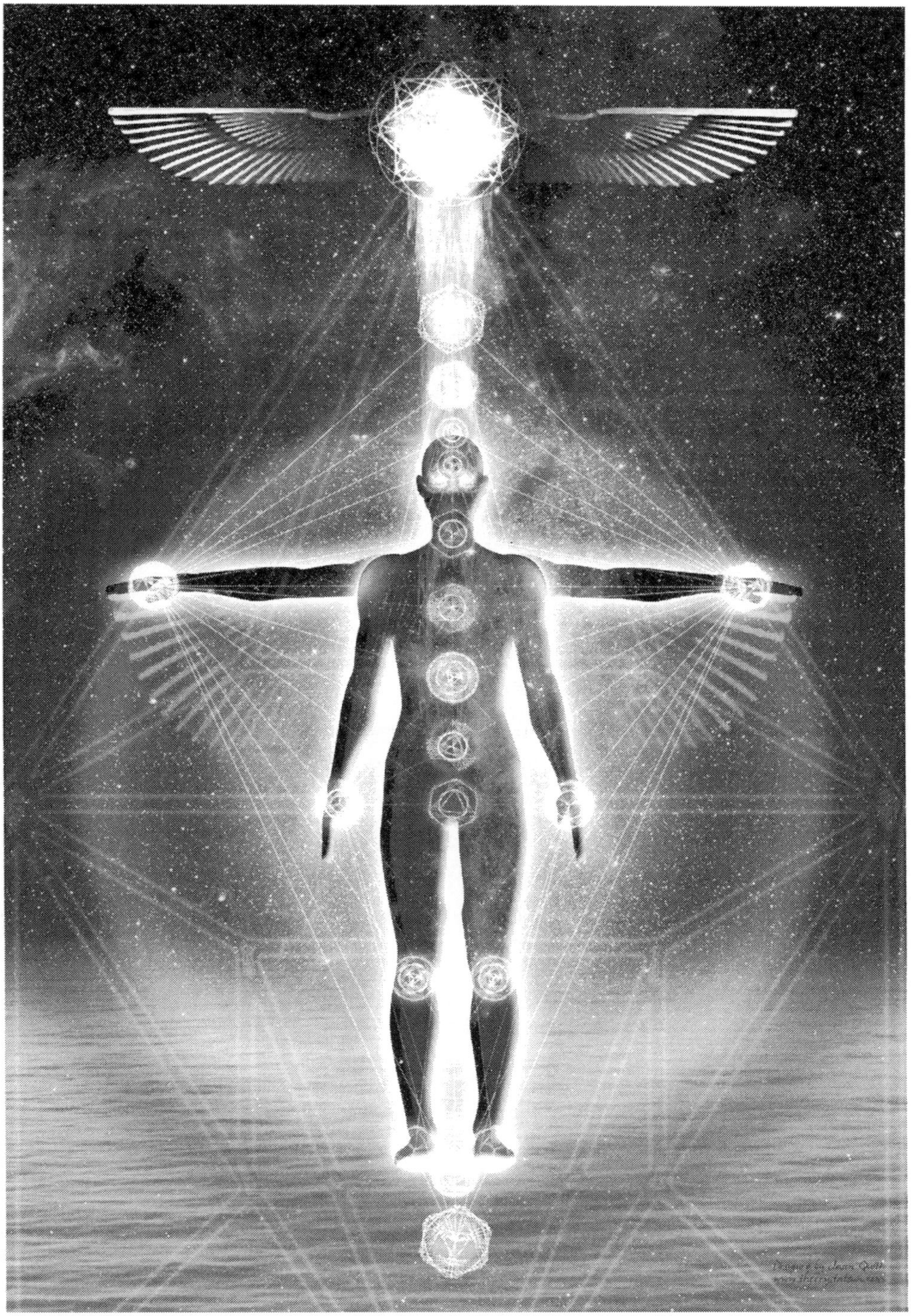

Jason Quitt's original artwork of the chakra systems.

Jason Quitt Biography

Jason would be considered a life long experiencer who has interacted with the multidimensional worlds.

Since an early age Jason has been awakened to things that are outside the normal range of perception of just the physical world. He has had many out of body experiences and has encountered ghosts, aliens and other dimensional beings. He has been taken on out of body time travel journeys and has remembered many of his past lives.

"In my early 20's, I started having terrifying experiences of sleep paralysis. I would be awakened by a presence in my room but I would be frozen and unable to wake myself up. These experiences started to happen more frequently and I started to become more and more conscious of what was going on. One night as I was trying very hard to shake myself out of this paralysis, something happened I wasn't expecting. I shook myself so hard that I popped out of my body and had my first out-of-body experience. As I came out of my body, I could see myself lying in bed frozen and there was a very tall being standing at the end of my bed. I knew that this was a genuine experience and was beyond my comprehension. From that moment on my perception of this world has shifted.

Ever since my first out-of-body experience, I found that under the right conditions I could leave my body and start to explore these new dimensions that had been opened to me. As I started to venture out into these new worlds, many different beings, guides, masters and energies started to come into my life. They would often wake me up and take me out of my body on journeys to many places and time lines to show and teach me many new things. I was no longer the same person after experiencing these journeys.

These beings gave me specific teachings to follow so I may live comfortably in this world. They said that the most important thing is to heal yourself, and only then could I effect change in others. Under their teachings and guidance I sought out many teachers and masters to receive wisdom and healing. Since then I have been given many powerful healing techniques and abilities to assist myself and others on the many paths of healing and enlightenment.

Since then, Jason has been studying various modalities and spiritual practices with teachers from around the world. He graduated from the Institute of Energy Wellness in 2005 and began working with ancient healing techniques and became a student of Algonquin Shamanism. From his out of body experiences Jason has received information on numerous energetic systems of healing and spiritual development. He published these methods in his book "Egyptian Postures of Power - Ancient Qigong System" and "The Yosef Codes - Sacred Geometry Mandalas of Meditation".

In 2015, Jason started to work on publishing his story and information with the late Bob Mitchell. "Forbidden Knowledge - Revelations of a Multidimensional Time Traveler" was released March 2016, and almost instantly went international being translated into German, Chinese and Japanese. Jason was also one of the guest personalities featured in the 2015 UFO documentary "The Resonance". Jason has also worked for Tesla Magazine from 2014-15.

www.thecrystalsun.com

Printed in Great Britain
by Amazon

56856598R00054